Between
the
Corn Rows

Between
the
Corn Rows

Stories of an Iowa Farm Family's Survival in the Great Depression

Robert Seltz

iUniverse, Inc.
Bloomington

Between The Corn Rows
Stories of an Iowa Farm Family's Survival
in the Great Depression

iUniverse books may be ordered through booksellers or by contacting:

iUniverse
1663 Liberty Drive
Bloomington, IN 47403
www.iuniverse.com
1-800-Authors (1-800-288-4677)

ISBN: 978-1-4759-3855-5 (sc)
ISBN: 978-1-4759-3857-9 (hc)
ISBN: 978-1-4759-3856-2 (e)

Printed in the United States of America

iUniverse rev. date: 7/27/2012

Dedication

To my brother Donald whose memory was of great help.

Contents

Foreword

If you google "Storytelling" you'll find there are over a hundred websites that are available. You'll also find that storytelling is one of the earliest forms of folk art. In recent years there's been a renewed interest in the art. Bob Seltz, in his book *Between The Corn Rows*, has proven that he is a talented storyteller.

Growing up as I did in the Great Depression, it was easy for me to resonate with the trials and tribulations of the members of the Schaub family, their extended family and neighbors. I could see our cupboard was often empty, and my mother would chide my father for squeezing the tea bag before she had a chance to brew a cup of tea for herself. I remember my father facetiously blaming me for causing the Depression as he packed a baloney sandwich for his lunch before leaving for work. What I wasn't prepared for was the vicarious feelings I had for Bob's stories of a family living on a farm in Iowa during that same period of time.

As a "city boy," all I knew about my father's job was that he worked in an insurance agency and made $28 a week. Dad would walk the two miles back and forth to work to save the ten cent fare for the trolley car. My mother had to give up her job at the telephone company when her boss found out she was pregnant with me. Our family's income was on my father's shoulders. Not so if you lived on a farm. Bob's stories made it crystal clear that farming was a "family business," a seven day a week partnership which was on the shoulders of each family member, but also often dependent on the weather. When I think of my chores as a boy, I think of cleaning up my room on Saturday and getting ten cents allowance, not getting up at the break of day and feeding the animals and coming home from school to face more chores before doing my homework.

I also became aware of how the spirit of cooperation among neighbors was often a matter of survival. I loved our little neighborhood. We might borrow a lawnmower from one of our neighbors, but living on a farm you might not only share a piece of equipment but also physically assist in harvesting crops if needed.

Many of Bob's stories are suspenseful, others are exciting and others work-a-day recollections of the reality of farm life. But whatever the pace of the stories, they all have "a moral to the story." Not like a preacher's story, although Bob's background as a pastor included years of preaching, but as a storyteller. And weren't Jesus' parables stories?

I'm happy to recommend *Between The Corn Rows* to you and hope you enjoy it as much as I did.

Donald F. Fausel, PhD.
Professor Emeritus, Arizona State University

Preface

Between The Corn Rows began as a family history for my kids and relatives describing events which occurred three quarters of a century ago. However, nearly forgotten memories of dramatic events began to spill out on the page. In the end I realized I was writing stories about my memories.

To protect identities I changed names and places and even added a number of characters. Also I expanded narratives to help them hang together. But in spite of taking such liberties I can say that most of the stories are based on actual events.

I'm glad *Between The Corn Rows* evolved into storytelling because it's a mode of communication that is powerful in conveying many things. It facilitates the sharing of cultural values and the teaching of honesty, respect and responsibility. One of the more important things about storytelling is that it helps us understand each other in spite of personal differences.

Storytelling has been around for a long time. There's a lot of it in the Bible, for example. I hope this little collection of stories will be a fitting way to share my memories not only with those who know me but also with anyone else who chooses to read it.

It's my wish to convey some of the spirit and drama, the comedy and tragedy of life on an Iowa farm in the decade of 1935 to 1945. May these pages inform as well as entertain.

Acknowledgments

It is my good fortune to have as a friend Dr. Donald Fausel, an author and former university professor. I owe him a large debt of thanks for editing my manuscript and making many helpful suggestions. He was always ready to listen, answer questions and offer encouragement.

I'm also grateful to my publisher for guidance, and to my family of origin who helped give birth to the stories related here.

Lastly, I deeply appreciate the love and support of my wife Janet.

Introduction

The story of the Schaub family opens when the oldest son boards a plane in 1990 to visit his aging parents back in Iowa. On the plane he falls asleep and has a dream about his childhood on the family farm. That dream constitutes a flashback highlighting events that took place decades earlier.

In the epilog four generations of the family come together for the oldest son's visit and celebrate those days of long ago. They remember well how both parents and children worked and played together from morning till night, somewhat removed from the rest of the world.

If you have spent time living on a farm you will recognize the unique lifestyle that is described in *Between The Corn Rows*. But if you have grown up in an urban setting you may find such a lifestyle strange and foreign at first, remembering how members of your family went their own way during the day and got together only in the evening. However, I suspect you may soon find yourself intrigued by many of the positive aspects of life on the farm and even identify vicariously with some of them.

Here are a few examples though not all of them are unique to farming.

A good deal of bonding takes place. The children bond closely with each other and also with neighbor kids—yes, even with animals. A similar phenomenon happens on the adult level, the parents developing a close relationship with nearby neighbors. In addition the churches help to hold the community together in a social and spiritual network.

Weather plays an important role in the success or failure of farming with storms and drought always a threat. The Schaubs are dependent on God, nature and good weather to enable them to support their family and attain their goals.

The children, often left on their own, creatively invent their entertainment and learn to be independent. Farming is a dangerous occupation though, and all too often accidents and injuries threaten from the sidelines. Somehow the children seem to manage well without utilities and other conveniences which their counterparts in the city take for granted.

Three challenges are constantly on the minds of the parents: get land, pay for it, and make a living from it. Consequently money concerns and financial insecurity are always lurking in the shadows. Regardless, the Schaubs would rather be between the corn rows than anywhere else.

Prologue

On a sunny July day in 1990 a small turbo-prop plane roared down the runway of the Minneapolis-St. Paul International airport. Quickly it rose into the cloudless sky. Nineteen passengers occupied every seat as they began a short flight to the city of Fort Dodge in northwest Iowa.

One of them, Dr. Ron Schaub, a distinguished looking physician in his mid-sixties, looked forward to visiting his aging parents who had recently entered an assisted living facility in Fort Dodge. The oldest of four children, Ron had graduated from medical school and moved to Cleveland, his wife's home town, where he established a practice in family medicine. Due to work commitments his wife Susan didn't accompany him on this trip.

Ron loosened his seat belt and gazed out the window at the fields of southern Minnesota.

The color green predominated as literally thousands of rows of corn and soybeans raced back and forth between the fences.

A smile crossed Ron's face as he thought back to his childhood on a farm southeast of Fort Dodge. Although it had been a wonderful way to grow up, he knew the kind of life he had experienced a half century earlier was gone forever. Everything had changed. He didn't even know the names of some of the huge machines the farmers were now piloting across their fields.

Beneath the plane he saw a large self-propelled combine gliding across an expansive yellow field of oats and harvesting a wide swath of grain. The driver sat in an air-conditioned cab enjoying his high-tech equipment and perhaps listening to music from his favorite CD. From high in the sky it looked so easy!

But Ron knew better. Farming in the 90's had to be done in a big way just to make a living. As small family farms gradually disappeared, corporate farms took their place. That was not surprising because of the daunting risks—drought, crop failures, high costs, low prices and large debts. Land and machinery cost ten to twenty times more in 1990 than they did fifty years earlier when Ron was a kid. *"Good thing I didn't stay on the farm,"* he mused. *"I'm not sure I would have had the faith and the guts that it takes."*

Because it was a long day of travel from Cleveland with two connecting flights, Ron began to feel sleepy. Again he looked out the window at the thousands of green rows far below, so plush and abundant. *"Farmers planted the seeds but only God could create that beautiful field,"* he thought.

Memories of things he did as a child began to flood his mind. His family walked through the rows pulling weeds. He and his brothers and sister hid in the rows playing hide and seek. In her older years his grandmother wandered into a field of tall corn and got lost.

Gradually Ron's eyes drifted shut and he fell asleep. Dreams and images of his childhood on the farm danced through his mind—so clearly that it seemed as if they were happening in that very moment...

1. Mother Nature

"Looks like something bad brewing out there in the west," thought Werner Schaub as he poured another bucket of corn into the hog feeder. Gusting winds and churning clouds were certainly not the kind of weather this tall Iowa farmer wanted. When a loud bolt of lightning struck nearby he jerked backward reflexively. Glancing toward the barn he saw nine-year-old Ron and seven-year-old Dale pitching hay into the cattle stalls.

"Hey guys," he shouted, "the sky's beginning to look angry. Run to the pasture and get the cows home while I finish feeding the hogs. It's gonna rain soon." Quickly they emerged from the barn. "Take Rex along. He knows how to speed things up."

"Okay Dad," said Ron. "Here Rex, come on fella!" The dog and the boys dashed toward the pasture and disappeared from sight.

Werner thought of himself as a calm and positive person, but on this humid June afternoon in 1935 he surely didn't feel that way. Instead, when the boys failed to return as soon as expected he became increasingly concerned.

He tried to reassure himself by recalling what a great dog Rex was. He knew his beloved white mongrel would grab the cattle's attention quickly even if they were preoccupied with eating grass. Barking, running back and forth, nipping at their hooves, Rex would get the cattle moving toward home in a hurry.

When it started to sprinkle Werner became even more worried. He ran toward the pasture but then spotted the cattle and the boys trotting toward the barn. "Thank God," he sighed as he noticed the sky was now almost as black as night—at only five thirty in the afternoon!

As the winds grew stronger dark clouds tinged with purple and orange from the hidden sun flew past swiftly. Startled by a loud blast of thunder, Werner ran into the barn pushing the last heifer ahead of him.

"What's that, Daddy?" asked Dale pointing out the barn door. Werner looked to the south and saw a huge black cloud that had dropped from the sky to the ground, moving eastward slowly and ominously. "My God, that looks wicked!" exclaimed Werner. "Come on, boys, let's get to the house!" The calmness that he tried to project now gave way to deep concern. Latching the barn door he grabbed the boys' hands and shouted, "Let's make a run for it." Just then the sprinkles turned into buckets of rain.

All three of them, soaking wet, burst into the house where the rest of the family was waiting anxiously—Laura, Werner's wife, and the two younger children, Sarah and Eddie, ages six and four. Quickly Werner and the boys shed their dripping bib overalls and put on dry clothes.

Though different than her husband, Laura complemented him. She was always pleased when he said he was blessed to have a wife who was not only strong but also sensitive. When she argued with his ideas he tried to take it in stride. Once he asked jokingly, "Honey, did your controlling mother teach you to be so strong?" They both had a good laugh.

"C'mon everyone," said Laura, "I've cooked a hot supper. Let's eat." Laura, like all the farming community, called the evening meal supper and the noon meal dinner. Lunch was just a snack eaten between meals. As they gathered around the table Laura continued, "It's such a stormy night. Dear, would you say a prayer?"

"Sure Honey," said Werner. With bowed head he thanked God for food and home and family, and especially for protection from the storm raging outside.

Laura was relieved when the kids began to laugh and argue as the kerosene lamp cast flickering shadows across their faces. She sensed that everyone's mood became a little lighter and things were normal again.

After supper she and Werner began reading the newspaper by the light of the same kerosene lamp. The kids turned to their toys and games. Although they and their neighbors didn't yet have electricity or running water, they did have a box telephone attached to the wall with a mouth piece protruding forward and a receiver hanging on a hook. Though it was awkward it did the job.

"I'm certainly glad we have a telephone on a night like this," Laura commented. "With our neighbors so far away it's almost a necessity. If only it wasn't a party line. I just hate the way nearly everyone listens to other people's conversations."

"The phone's been busy," said Werner. "I wonder if people are talking about the storm tonight."

Suddenly there was a call for the Schaubs—one long ring and one short. Werner took the receiver off the hook and said hello.

"Hi Werner, it's me," said a familiar voice. Werner was glad to hear from his good friend George McDonald, a kind and helpful neighbor who lived less than a mile down the road. "You folks surviving the weather?" asked George.

"We're doing okay, but the sky sure looked bad a while ago. The phone's been ringin' a lot too. You heard anything?"

"Yup. A tornado touched down near the highway south of here a little before six. Traveled almost five miles before it lifted. It was a bad one, wiped out some homes."

"O my God! Anyone injured?"

"I don't know but I'd like to drive over there tomorrow morning and take a look. Wanna go? I thought maybe we could help. My son Tom is eager to go. Your boys could come along too."

"Sounds good to me. I know my boys will want to go if Tom does. What time shall we be at your place?"

"How about nine o'clock?"

"Okay, see you then."

After a few seconds of silence George suggested, "Let's say a prayer for those folks along the highway. I'm afraid of what we're going to see."

George's fears were well founded. Early the next morning the radio news programs described in detail the "devastating tornado" which had ripped through Webster County, possibly the worst that had ever hit the area. George, Werner and the three boys drove south to the paved highway and turned west. Shocked by the destruction confronting them on all sides, George exclaimed, "Oh Lord, it looks like a war zone!" A World War I vet, he had fought in the trenches of France so his remark was not just a cliché.

Debris was everywhere. Trees, stripped of bark and torn up by their roots, lay on the ground with large branches snapped like twigs. Telephone poles leaned sideways or, broken in half, dangled helplessly from their wires.

"Look at that!" cried Dale pointing to an adjacent field where three cattle had died. One cow's horns plunged forcefully into the ground, its neck obviously broken. In another field a vehicle and a refrigerator crashed together with pieces of metal and wood scattered all around. Crops lay flattened as far as the eye could see. "This gives me a sick feeling in the pit of my stomach," whispered George.

He drove his car into a driveway where he noticed a number of people had gathered to survey the destruction. What formerly had been a house, crib, barn, and other smaller buildings was now a massive field of boards, tin, glass, shingles and dead animals. Several confused chickens and hogs continued to walk around in a daze with fear in their eyes. The smell of dust and garbage filled the air while gray clouds still swirled in the sky above.

"Can you believe this?" exclaimed Ron as he showed the others several stems of straw protruding like nails from the bark of a tree. "What kind of wind could do that?" he asked.

Joining a group of others they listened to a man who had survived the tornado and was sharing his experience. Still shaken, he stumbled over his words and tried to hold back his tears. "It was just horrible," he mumbled. Pointing to a heap of boards and twisted metal a short distance down the highway, he continued, "That used to be our house! When we saw the black cloud coming my family and I ran down into the storm cellar. We peeked through a crack in the door and were shocked by what we saw. If it hadn't been for that tiny shelter in the ground all of us would've been goners." He stopped briefly, his body quivering.

"All at once we heard a loud twisting noise. Before we knew what was happening our house was gone—it just disappeared! We saw a lot of stuff flying all around. Looking outside we saw the storm heading toward this place here where we're standing now. I know it's hard to believe, but this house went straight up into the air and then exploded into a million pieces. Oh my God! It was awful! But then a minute later it got completely quiet."

By now tears were running down the man's face, and everyone else's too. It was an emotional day.

George, Werner and the boys walked over to a large cavity which had been the basement of the house. It was empty except for a few household items left behind. "How can nature be so cruel?" asked Tom.

"Nature doesn't have any feelings," answered George. "It just reacts to conditions in the atmosphere without worrying about whether or not it's fair."

"But why does God *allow* nature to do something like this?" Tom persisted.

"I wish I could answer that but I can't," said George. "Let's just pray God helps these people."

"Maybe our churches could do something," Werner interjected. "Let's suggest we have an offering of food and money."

The McDonald family attended a Roman Catholic church and the Schaubs belonged to a rural Lutheran congregation several miles southeast of Fort Dodge. Many Irish Catholics and German Lutherans lived intermingled in that part of rural Iowa, generally respecting each other and getting along well. Often they worked together, especially during the oats harvest when they shared one large threshing machine and moved from farm to farm. Occasionally they hurled religious or nationalistic stereotypes at each other, but for the most part it was simply neighbors having fun and teasing one another.

"That's a great idea," said George. The suggestion caught on and later several local churches joined in the effort to assist their neighbors.

George and Werner heard clapping erupting from the group of people standing in the driveway. They walked over to see what was going on. Someone had just brought word that miraculously only one person died as a result of the tornado, though several others sustained injuries. "Most of the people must have seen the storm approaching and fled to their basements or storm cellars in time," commented Werner.

The man who died drove west on the highway and unwittingly ran right into the tornado. It swept up his vehicle and threw it into a field.

"I wonder if he was in that smashed car we saw," said Dale.

As the five of them started to drive home they decided to check out the wreckage in the field. Parking at the side of the road, they climbed over what was left of the fence and began walking toward the wreck. Strangely, they heard music in the distance which sounded like a cowboy moaning about his lost love.

"What's that!" exclaimed Ron. Hearing such a sound in a deserted field gave them all an eerie feeling.

As they got closer to the vehicle they could see it was a pickup truck. *The music got louder!* When they reached the site of the wreck George said, "The music seems to be coming from the truck radio. I'll bet it's still tuned to the station the driver was listening to just before he died."

"You're right," replied Werner. "This poor old pickup is a total wreck but the radio and battery are still working!"

Overwhelmed and intimidated by what they had experienced, the group didn't say much on the way back. When George and Tom reached home, Werner and the two boys transferred to their car and proceeded toward their place. Finally Ron broke the silence and asked, "Dad, could something like that ever happen to our house?"

"Not likely," Werner replied. "Tornados don't strike often and don't cover a large area, so the odds are in our favor. But then again, you never know. By the way our house is not exactly *our* house. We're renters, you know."

"Will we ever own our own home?" asked Ron.

"I certainly hope so," replied Werner. "I'm praying that someday we can buy our own house, our own farm, and our own buildings. That's my dream, my biggest goal in life. However, there's a big problem standing in the way."

"What's that?"

"It requires a lot of money."

Later that evening after the family finished supper and a lot of conversation about the tornado, Dale and his brother went outside.

"Wow, look at the sky!" exclaimed Ron. "The clouds are breaking up just enough to let the sun peek through. Aren't those colors pretty?"

Pools of water lay everywhere from the rain the night before. The temperature felt cool, the air smelled clean, and the vegetation seemed invigorated.

"How about launching our raft?" suggested Dale.

The boys had built a raft recently using discarded lumber piled in the machinery shed. Arranging the boards in a crisscross fashion and nailing them together, they created an awkward vessel measuring about six by eight feet. Though very heavy, they managed to drag it to a pond in the south pasture using ropes. A low area in the pasture had filled with water during the storm creating a tiny lake. With a little effort the boys got the raft afloat. Each took a long wood pole and jumped on the raft, inviting Rex to come along. Pushing out with their poles, they quickly glided to the center of the pond.

"Hey, this is great," exclaimed Ron. "It floats beautifully." It helped that the boys weren't very heavy, and since Dale was tall for his age they were almost the same size and weight.

By this time their tomboyish younger sister Sarah had come to the pasture to see if she could join the fun. Boldly she waved to them from the water's edge. With pride in their accomplishment Ron and Dale waved back. Making their way to the grassy shore they motioned Sarah to jump on board. Then they pushed out again.

Awe-struck by the beauty of the evening, the three kids and Rex floated quietly. A bright orange hue of the setting sun flooded the western horizon while a few remaining clouds broke the light into many shades of purple and yellow. It was quiet except for a gentle splash of the water, a croaking frog nearby, and a faint song from a distant bird.

"It's really pretty tonight, isn't it?" commented Sarah.

"It sure is," answered Dale.

"It's a lot different from last night, that's for sure," said Ron.

Unconsciously the kids had learned something important about Mother Nature. She had two distinct faces. One could be violent and destructive like the previous evening. The other, like tonight, could be beautiful, serene and peaceful.

That's a truth which the children and indeed the whole farm community would experience again and again.

2. Land is Gold

The old black Chevy, surrounded by a cloud of dust, roared down the gravel lane toward the house. Werner jumped out of the car and ran up the porch steps and through the front door. "Hey Honey, are you here?" he shouted.

"I'm here," came the reply from the kitchen.

"You'll never guess what happened this morning."

"I wouldn't even try. Would you like a cup of coffee while you tell me about it?" Laura asked, trying to calm her husband down.

"Sure, thanks. I think it's good news. I drove to Webster City this morning to buy some weed spray. On Senaca Street I saw our landlord, Bill Latham. Jokingly I said, 'I suppose you'll be expecting a rent check one of these days.' His answer surprised me. 'Why pay rent when you can *own* the land? Would you like to buy it?' 'Are you serious?' I asked, and he said, 'I'm very serious. My wife and I would like to retire and move closer to our daughter and grandchildren in South Carolina. So we've decided to sell the 160 acres you're renting plus another 80 acres I own two miles farther west. You've been an excellent tenant and I'd like to give you a chance to own both properties if you're interested. However it's going to be an auction sale and you'd have to be ready to make a bid.'"

"That *is* surprising," said Laura. "How did you respond?"

"Frankly I was so shocked I didn't know what to say at first. I told him it had always been our hope to own a farm but we weren't sure we could afford it, let alone get a mortgage."

"Would that be out of the question?" asked Laura.

"I'm afraid so. Bill said he needs to get at least $100 per acre. That would be $24,000 for 240 acres. I doubt we could be approved for a loan that big. Even if my dad helped us with a down payment I'm afraid we still couldn't handle the mortgage payments."

"That makes sense," replied Laura, the careful and financially conservative member of the family. She knew Werner would be eager to buy the land if he thought there was any way they could afford it. Gradually a wrinkle appeared on her brow and a slight smile at the corners of her mouth.

"A penny for your thoughts," said Werner.

"Well, I was wondering what would happen if we talked with both your father and my mother about this opportunity. You know my mother. When she puts her mind to something it usually happens!"

"That's for sure," replied Werner with a knowing grin. "If *she* got behind us, we just might be able to pull it off." After reflecting for a few seconds he continued, "Tell you what; I'll talk with my dad first and see what he says, and then we'll put all the facts on paper and have a visit with your parents. Sound okay?"

"Sounds good to me," answered Laura as she gathered the cups and saucers. Tending to be optimistic, she believed that things often work out if one keeps praying and never gives up. "When will you talk with your dad?" she asked.

"I'll phone him right away. It might be a long time before we get another opportunity as good as this one."

For Laura's sake as well as his own, Werner tried to be positive as he cranked the little handle on the phone box. Far from certain their plan would work, he gave his father's number to the operator with a bit of apprehension.

Dr. Carl Schaub picked up the phone in his medical office in Sioux City, Iowa, a city more than a hundred miles west of Werner's home located near the point where the borders of South Dakota,

Nebraska and Iowa meet. In addition to his private family practice Dr. Schaub served on the staff of the hospital in Sioux City. He had helped Werner get a job as an orderly at that hospital during his teen years. Having speculated in land purchases himself, Dr. Schaub understood very well the challenges that his son was considering in the purchase of a farm, so the cautious doctor had many questions. After about fifteen minutes of conversation Werner hung up the phone.

"Well, what did he say?" asked Laura impatiently.

Werner seemed stunned. "I can't believe it. Dad said okay."

"Okay what?"

"He said he would be willing to loan us $3,000 for a down payment. If things pan out he expects the money to be paid back. But if not, he hinted he might forgive some of the loan and jokingly said he wouldn't foreclose. I'm amazed!"

Werner's surprise resulted from growing up with a father who was stern and principled in financial matters but fair and honest to the core. Dr. Schaub's family possessed deep religious and moral values which may have led to Werner's Uncle Harry, his dad's brother, becoming a Lutheran pastor. Integrity was considered to be of paramount importance when it came to the use of money or anything else of value.

Werner remembered well an experience which he and one of his sisters had as young kids. Their father gave each of them a dime for the Sunday School offering. With candy rarely available in their home, the two of them conspired to stop at a store and get something sweet. Each bought a five cent candy bar which left the remaining nickel for the Sunday School offering, a reasonable compromise they thought. Unfortunately their crime was discovered and they got a spanking and no money or allowance for a month. This distant memory caused Werner to feel especially grateful for the generous offer his father now made.

"That's wonderful!" exclaimed Laura. "I had a feeling your Dad would come through. But now we've got to talk with *my* parents and to say the least, that could be more challenging."

Laura knew that her mother, Helena Bauer, also called Grandma Bauer by those who knew her well, was an unusual woman. Blessed with strength and intelligence, she might be kind and polite one moment and hard as nails the next. When she worked in the fields or pulled weeds between the rows, her husband could hardly keep up with her. Ambition, endurance and determination were woven into the fabric of her being.

"I'm well aware of the dynamics between me and my mother," Laura stated. "I'll never forget some of the experiences which forged both of us into the people we are today."

When Helena was in her late teens in the latter part of the nineteenth century, she asked her father if he would help her get a farm just as he had helped her brothers. "No, Helena," he answered, "that's for men, not women. Someday your future husband will buy a farm for both of you."

Helena was furious. She argued with her father on the grounds of fairness, but to no avail. Privately she shed a few tears in her bedroom where no one could see her. The last thing she wanted was to show any sign of weakness. Recovering quickly, she made a solemn vow that she would get a farm on her own—someday, somehow.

When a friend and distant relative invited Helena to come to Chicago for a visit, she bought a train ticket and headed for the "Windy City." While there she met a strong young man named Klaus Bauer who had recently immigrated from Germany. Before she returned to Iowa the two of them were engaged. She persuaded Klaus that hard work would eventually enable them to buy their own farm. Improbable as it may seem, that's exactly what happened.

It was fortunate for Helena that her husband was a kind and good man with an easy going spirit. Though he usually deferred to her, he could be very strong when it was required. Whenever he thought she had crossed the line of reason and common sense, he challenged her sternly. At such times, amazingly, she retreated into silence which bespoke agreement even though she was too proud to admit it.

After renting some land and working side by side for several years, they were able to buy a small 80 acre farm. Helena overflowed with joy when she finally achieved her dream of owning her own farm—*without* her father's help! Laura and her brother Albert grew up on this farm which later expanded when their parents acquired more land.

—∞∞—

Early in her childhood Laura had a few formative experiences with her mother which seared indelible imprints in her spirit. As an adult she realized that those experiences, though very painful at the time, made her a stronger person than she may otherwise have become.

For example, one cold day in October Helena and Klaus prepared for a day of corn picking in the field. Since they didn't yet have tractors and harvesters but only horses and wagons, they had to pick each ear of corn by hand—very tedious work!

"What about Laura and Albert?" asked Klaus. "They're too young to be left alone."

"I'll give them some food and toys and lock them in the upstairs of the house," replied Helena. "They'll be safe there and shouldn't get into any trouble."

Klaus didn't feel good about her decision but reluctantly agreed.

Several hours proved to be a long time for the children to wait for their parents' return. After a while they began to feel cold and lonely. Finally Laura said, "I'm getting out of here."

"How?" asked Albert.

"I'll crawl out the window to the roof. From there I can climb down the branches of the maple tree. Then I'll come back inside the house and unlock the door to the stairs so you can come down too."

Laura's plan worked perfectly except Albert hesitated because he knew there would be "hell" to pay later. But finally he relented and joined Laura downstairs.

Toward evening they were having fun when suddenly they heard the ominous sound of horses and a wagon loaded with corn and rumbling toward the crib. They shuddered as their mother approached the house. Helena, shocked and angry at what had transpired, gave the kids a hard spanking and sent them *back* upstairs—to bed.

⸺

Laura would never forget one other painful experience with her mother. On a summer day when she was about seven years old she helped Helena pull weeds between the rows of a small soybean field. Suddenly tripping and falling over a large rock, Laura felt a sharp pain in her right leg and couldn't put any weight on it. "I think it's broken!" she cried.

"Probably it's just a bad bruise," said her mother as she tore strips of cloth from her apron and tied two small sticks of wood tightly to the sides of Laura's leg. "There, that's a good splint. Now go home and lie down until I get there."

"But it hurts a lot, Mama."

"Go slow, Laura. You're a strong girl. You can make it," replied her mother.

Spotting another piece of wood lying nearby, Laura picked it up and used it as a crutch. She limped home and lay on her bed crying until mercifully she fell asleep. Two hours later Helena finally came home with a different attitude, solicitous and kind.

"Here Laura, take this small aspirin," she said. "Then we're going to wrap your leg with a better splint."

Since Helena didn't consult a doctor it was indeed fortunate the leg had not been fractured. It was cracked and bruised however. Though the healing and pain lasted only about ten days, Laura never forgot the lonely and painful trek home that summer afternoon, a hobbling journey she had to make all by herself.

It's likely such experiences resulted in Laura's becoming a strong and independent young woman. Klaus had a totally different personality. Considering his little girl a gift from God, he gave her the love she so desperately needed .

One evening at bedtime Laura pleaded, "Daddy, would you sing one of your happy German songs?" She loved his soft German accent and gentle manner. He frequently hugged and reassured her, especially when Helena was on the war path. As an adult Laura realized she inherited strength from her mother, but she also understood the debt she owed her father for her sense of wholeness and self-esteem.

⚬⚬⚬

"I guess we should phone your parents," said Werner. "I nominate you for the job."

Laura agreed and placed the call. Helena responded with a cheery hello.

"Hi Mom. Werner and I have a request. If it's okay with you and Dad, we'd like to drive over and have a talk with both of you tonight."

"That sounds mysterious. What's on your mind?"

"We'd like to discuss the possibility of buying some farm land."

"My goodness, that's exciting. Sure, come on over."

As they drove toward the Bauer home their hearts began to beat a little faster than normal. Upon arrival they felt relieved to find Helena in a rather upbeat mood. After a few pleasantries they explained the new developments—their landlord's plan to sell his two pieces of land in an auction and Dr. Schaub's willingness to help with a $3,000 down payment. When they finished they waited nervously for a response.

"That's a wonderful opportunity," said Klaus.

"It certainly is," added Helena, remembering how hurt and disappointed she felt when her father refused to help her buy land. To Laura's surprise her mother seemed enthusiastic about the prospect of helping her daughter and son-in-law achieve a goal which she and Klaus had to accomplish by themselves. In unison Laura and Werner breathed a sigh of relief.

"I have a confession to make," said Helena. "Klaus and I heard rumors about that land sale and we did a little investigating. We've been trying to think of ways we could help you get some of that land, or all of it. I hope you don't mind."

"Oh no, we appreciate that, Mom," replied Laura.

"Yes we do," said Werner with a slight frown between his eyes. "I must admit I'm a little uncomfortable with your taking the lead. We should be doing that ourselves—with your help perhaps."

"He's right," said Klaus. "You two can veto anything you want. We can't guarantee our plan would work anyway."

"That's true," continued Grandma Bauer. By now almost everyone called her that. "But would you like to hear our plan anyway?"

"Certainly," they replied.

"We thought we'd attend the auction and try to purchase the land ourselves. If we succeed we'll transfer the title of the 80 acres to the two of you. Technically you'd owe us the money, but we'd forgive part or all of that debt in the future when we divide our assets between Albert and Laura. How does that sound so far?"

"It sounds great," agreed Werner. "But what about the 160 acres we're renting now? If we don't get that we'll have to move out and find another place to rent."

"If we also manage to buy that, we'll turn around and sell it to the two of you. I know you're worried about being approved for a mortgage but I think the bank will like the looks of that $3,000 your father is willing to loan for the down payment. That will lower the debt for the 160 acres from about $16,000 to $13,000. I'm quite sure they'll give you the mortgage for that amount."

"The bank knows we intend to support you," added Klaus. Werner and Laura appreciated that special word of reassurance from Klaus because he seldom said much when Helena was present. Usually she did most of the talking.

"The success of our plan depends on two things," added Grandma Bauer. "First we'll have to win the bidding at the two auctions which may not be easy. And then the two of you will have to make a total commitment to meet the mortgage payments. Can you do that?"

"We sure can," stated Werner trying to appear confident. "Your plan is good and we're grateful for your willingness to help. We'll do everything possible to hold up our end of the deal, won't we Honey?"

"Absolutely," she replied.

While sharing cake and coffee with the Bauers Laura and Werner thanked them again for their help and generosity. After a few goodbyes they returned to their car and drove home, happy and excited but also more than a little scared.

The next morning Werner, invigorated by a deep blue sky and fresh air, began moving farm equipment into the storage shed. The work wasn't urgent but it helped him escape the concerns burdening his mind. He couldn't help feeling overwhelmed by the huge commitment he and Laura made the previous evening.

"What if the auction didn't turn out as planned?" he wondered. *"If it did would they get the mortgage? If so would they be able to make the payments?"* It helped that Dale tagged along, helping and asking a lot of questions.

One task remained: hitching a team of horses to a wagon and pulling it into the shed. Werner drove the horses to a closed gate. Turning to Dale he asked, "Do you think you can hold the reins while I jump out and open the gate?"

"Sure Dad." Dale felt proud whenever given adult responsibilities.

As Werner began unlatching the gate Dale's curiosity shifted into high gear. *"Are the reins long enough to reach the back of the wagon box?"* he wondered. Moving backward with the reins he discovered they were about one foot too short. *"Maybe if I pull them a little harder they'll reach the back,"* he reasoned. As he did so the bits jerked in the horses' mouths. Though generally calm, both horses were startled by the jerk and immediately bolted through the opened gate. Werner watched helplessly. He shouted loudly "Whoa!" to no avail.

Each horse fed off the fright of the other as their speed escalated. They bypassed the shed and sped into an open pasture with the wagon and Dale bouncing and rattling behind. Werner saw Dale's cap fly off and his blond hair blowing in the wind. Shocked and frightened, he began running through a cloud of dust toward the wagon. The horses dashed into a soft plowed field casting loose dirt high into the air. Next they circled back toward home with the wagon and its precious cargo following behind—but on two wheels, leaving the other two spinning approximately one foot in the air!

"Oh my God, please stop them!" cried Werner as he saw the horses and wagon speeding directly toward the fence which separated the field and the pasture. Fortunately it wasn't a barbed wire fence. The team and wagon burst through the fence as though it weren't even there. By this time Werner was running across the pasture on a collision course with the horses. He stopped, threw his arms into the air and shouted "Whoa!" as loudly as he could. Miraculously the horses slowed to a trot. He managed to grab the bridle of one horse and pulled its head forcefully down to the ground. That forced the team to slow down to a walk and they finally stopped.

Frozen with fear, Werner wondered if Dale had been hurt. "Are you all right?" he yelled.

"Yup, I'm okay," Dale replied. "It was kinda fun—but I lost my good cap!"

Werner breathed a sigh of relief and a prayer of thanks to God. His legs were trembling with fright. "Don't worry about your cap," he said. "I'll get you a brand new one!"

Knowing it was mostly his own fault, Werner didn't scold Dale for his experiment with the reins. He realized too late that it had been careless of him to leave his seven-year-old son alone in a wagon hitched to a team of fresh horses. *Farming isn't the safest occupation for either kids or adults,* he thought.

When he and Dale made their way back to the house they described their harrowing adventure. Obviously upset, Laura gave her husband a stern lecture on child safety and the necessity of using good judgment with children. As for Dale, he believed his dad had done a terrific job of stopping the horses and felt the whole experience was exciting.

Quickly Laura moved to another subject. "My mother phoned and told me that Bill Latham has scheduled the farm auction for the last Saturday in August, just two weeks from now."

"That's sooner than I imagined," said Werner, "but I'm glad because I don't like worrying about it."

"Mother also said a problem has arisen."

"Oh? What's that?"

"She heard her cousin Gustav Meier is also planning to make a bid for our 160 acres. His farm is only a couple miles away and he feels it would be a good way for him to enlarge his operation."

"Bad luck!" growled Werner. "Did your mother tell him about our plans?"

"No, she hasn't talked to him yet but she's planning to phone him. They aren't the best of friends, you know."

Werner wanted to phone Grandma Bauer right away but he was concerned about the lack of privacy on the party line, so he decided to drive to her house instead. When he arrived he asked her, "Have you talked with Gustav yet?"

"Yes, I phoned and asked what his plans were. He said he's hoping to buy the 160 acres because he needs more land for his sons. He added that if he were successful he would allow you and Laura to stay on the farm until the first of March. You could harvest your crops this fall and hopefully find another place to rent by next spring. Wasn't that generous of him to allow you to harvest your own crops?" Grandma Bauer asked sarcastically.

"Yes, very kind."

"I'm not surprised. He's an ill-tempered man, not my favorite relative."

"Did you mention anything to him about our plans?"

"No I didn't. I want to think things through carefully and try to figure out the best way to proceed. If you have any ideas give me a call, okay?"

"Okay. I don't have any right now but I'll give it a lot of thought."

"Try not to worry and tell Laura the same. I think our plan can still work."

That was good advice but it didn't help much. The next several days Laura and Werner had many discussions about their future, trying to hide their concern from the children as much as possible. Laura phoned her mother a few times but got only reassurances, nothing definite. Just a few days before the auction the phone rang—a long and a short.

"Hi Werner, this is Helena. I just wanted to tell you that I have a revised plan that might succeed. I'll tell you more later but I need to talk with a few people first to see if I can count on them. Can you trust me on this one?"

"At this point I don't have much choice. Go ahead."

"Good! If not before I'll see you at the auction Saturday morning at ten sharp and fill you in then. Remember, try not to worry. I'm optimistic."

"Okay, thanks Helena," said Werner somberly as he hung up the phone.

Both Laura and Werner were anxious but strangely calm the day before the auction. Together they tried to resign themselves to whatever Helena—and God—had in mind. The question they could not escape was: "What's Grandma Bauer up to?"

When Saturday morning arrived all six members of the Schaub family climbed out of bed earlier than usual, quickly finished their chores and ate breakfast. With anticipation and a little dread they crowded into the Chevy and headed for Bill Latham's 80 acre section of land, the appointed site of the auction.

Though they arrived early Werner noticed Helena and Klaus were already there. The crisp morning air felt good in his lungs and the rising sun promised it would be a beautiful day. Near a makeshift podium several rows of chairs formed a semicircle. The

Bauers and Schaubs found a place to sit while the kids teamed up with a few of their friends and began to run and play. Nearby corn seven feet high waved in the breezes.

"What's your game plan?" asked Werner.

"The first order of business is to get this smaller property," replied Helena. Klaus will do the bidding and I think everything will turn out fine for us."

At last the auctioneer stepped up to a makeshift podium and shuffled his papers. After welcoming everyone he described the boundaries of both properties in a humorless disinterested manner—just another day's work for him. But for Werner and Laura it was a crucial day because their future was hanging in the balance.

The 80 acres sold quickly since the smaller acreage commanded less interest. Klaus won the bidding at just $95 per acre. Laura's heart began to beat with joy.

"That was great!" exclaimed Werner. "Let's hope the next auction goes as well."

"Ya, let's hope," said Klaus.

After a little more paper shuffling the auctioneer continued by declaring, "We'll start the bidding for Mr. Latham's 160 acre property at $85 per acre. Do I have any offers?" With that he began his speed-talk in true auctioning style. Without hesitation four people jumped into the process: a farmer from a neighboring county, an attorney from Webster City by the name of Bert Dickson, Helena's cousin Gustav Meier, and Klaus. Everyone knew Klaus spoke not only for himself but also for Helena. Nevertheless the act of bidding for land was done by men, not women.

After all four persons made a couple bids, each one raising the others' by just a little, Mr. Dickson shouted loudly, "$100 per acre!" At this point the farmer from the neighboring county fell silent and dropped out. To everyone's amazement, so did Klaus!

A look of shock and disappointment crossed Werner's face. "What's going on here?" he whispered to Laura. "Why would your parents back out now?"

"I don't know," she answered as a tear ran down her cheek. In her mind she could see their home and livelihood slipping away.

It was clear Gustav was surprised and confused too. Naturally he didn't want to raise the bidding much higher. Not quite sure what to do, he quickly wrote a note, folded it and asked his son to give it to Mr. Dickson. The note read, "If you win the bid would you be willing to sell at a good profit?"

"Is that legal?" asked his son.

"I'm not sure but hurry and give it to him anyway!"

Mr. Dickson looked at the note and jotted on it, "I can't answer that."

Werner noticed the quick note exchange and said to Helena, "Did you see that? I wonder if Gustav tried to make a sly arrangement with Dickson on the side."

"It looks suspicious," she agreed.

The auctioneer intoned, "I have a bid of $100 per acre. Will anyone raise it?"

Gustav concluded that the vagueness of Dickson's note implied that he *would* be open to a deal later. However to make everything appear normal he thought he should make one more offer. "I bid $105," he yelled.

"$110!" Mr. Dickson shot back.

"$110," said the auctioneer. "Is there another offer?"

No one responded. Everything was silent except for the soft rustling of corn leaves in the breeze.

Finally the auctioneer pounded the gavel on the podium and declared that Mr. Latham's 160 acre property was sold to Mr. Dickson at a price of $110 per acre.

Shortly thereafter Werner saw Gustav approach the attorney and speak privately with him. He became increasingly agitated and said to Laura and the Bauers, "Look at that! I'm sure Gustav is trying to make a deal with Dickson. He's still trying to get our farm." Laura struggled to hold back her emotions.

"Don't panic," replied Helena. "We'll have a talk with Dickson ourselves."

Almost on cue Dickson turned and began walking toward them. When he arrived Werner said, "Mr. Dickson, I must tell you I'm very concerned about your discussion with Gustav Meier."

"Why is that?"

"To be honest I'm worried he was trying to make a deal with you to get our farm."

"As a matter of fact you're right. He said he needed the land for his sons. He offered to give me $800, or $5 per acre more than I paid, if I would turn around and sell it to him. I said I'd like to help him but a few days earlier I had received a similar proposal from someone else. He wanted to know who made the proposal, so I told him."

"Would you also tell me?" asked Werner. "The future of my family is at stake."

"I thought you knew. It was your parents-in-law, Helena and Klaus."

Shock and surprise hit Werner so hard it left him speechless.

"I'll see you at the County Court House to sign the papers," stated Dickson. Then he said goodbye to everyone and left.

Meanwhile Gustav was struggling to comprehend what the attorney had just told him. His face turned red with anger. Could it be that his own cousin had outsmarted him and snatched the land from his grasp? How frustrating to realize that in the future it would not be his sons who farmed the 160 acres. Instead it would be the son-in-law of his less than favorite cousin Helena. At that moment he didn't want to consider the fact that Werner had already been renting the land for a number of years.

Without pausing to think rationally Gustav walked toward the Bauers. "That was really a nasty trick, Helena, even for someone like you!" snarled Gustav. "You should be ashamed!"

"Listen Gustav, I did the same thing you yourself tried to do," countered Helena. "Don't be a sore loser. We both wanted the farm but only one of us could have it."

"It was a rotten way to do business," growled Gustav as he stormed away.

In his heart he knew Helena was right in saying he had attempted the same "nasty trick," but that didn't prevent a deep strain in their relationship. Ironically, several years later Helena helped facilitate another land purchase, this time for Gustav, which gave him additional land not far from his home. That took some of the scab off the wound but the strain never healed completely.

Helena had more explaining to do.

"Mother, why in the world didn't you tell us about your scheme?" demanded Laura.

"At least we could have helped," added Werner. "To tell the truth it's embarrassing to have my mother-in-law do my so-called 'nasty work' for me."

"I know, I know," answered Helena. "First, I didn't have much time to put the pieces together, and second, I knew you would be worried and might even resist me. Just be glad it worked. Otherwise you'd have to move now and find another farm to rent."

Laura and Werner had to admit they were happy about that. Their "impossible" dream of owning a farm was actually coming to fruition as all of them had planned and hoped from the beginning.

The next few days proved to be busy ones at the bank and County Court House in Fort Dodge. As promised, Helena and Klaus completed the paper work on the west 80 acres and immediately transferred the title to Laura and Werner. At $95 per acre that amounted to a debt of $7,600—or possibly an inheritance gift later. Next the Bauers helped them secure a mortgage from the bank so they could purchase the 160 acres from Mr. Dickson. The total cost at $110 per acre was $17,600. Laura and Werner made a down payment of $3,000, the amount loaned to them by Werner's father. That left them with a mortgage debt of $14,600—a big but manageable challenge for the young couple. However Werner assumed responsibility also for the debts he owed to his father and the Bauers. He wasn't aware that Helena paid Mr. Dickson extra for his services.

Werner felt three huge challenges facing him and Laura: making a living, raising four children, and repaying the debts. All this they would strive to do in the wake of a world-wide depression. He knew difficult days lay ahead, but hopefully happy ones too.

That evening all four kids decided to celebrate their family's good fortune by taking a sunset cruise on the raft. It was disappointing when they arrived at the pond and found most of the water gone. Lack of rain, evaporation and thirsty soil had taken a toll in recent days leaving too little water for a cruise.

"No fair!" said Sarah and Eddie.

"Yeah, we need more rain," said Dale.

Looking over the brown dry grass in the pasture, Ron added, "I'll bet Dad feels the same way."

3. School Days

The Schaub children had mixed feelings as the fall of 1935 approached because it meant summer vacation would end soon and school would start again. But there was an upside to the beginning of a new school year. Laura and the kids had a tradition of going shopping for clothes and other needed items for school. Working with a tight budget she planned the shopping spree carefully.

"Where shall we go this year, Webster City or Fort Dodge?" asked Laura.

"Let's go to Fort Dodge. They have good milk shakes there," answered Sarah.

The kids loved a place in Fort Dodge that they considered the best ice cream shop in Webster County. Its specialty was large thick milk shakes for just fifteen cents each.

The next morning Laura and the kids got into the Chevy and drove to Fort Dodge. After buying a few school supplies they went to a discount clothing store.

"Now remember our agreement," cautioned Laura. "Each of you gets one new pair of tennis shoes and one new outfit. Sarah can select a blouse and skirt and you boys can choose a shirt and a pair of overalls. Okay?"

"Okay Mom, we know," said Dale with resignation in his voice.

"Me too, Mommy? Even if I don't go to school yet?" pleaded Eddie.

"Yes Eddie, you get the same as the others."

When the children attended school Laura made sure they wore clothes that were either new or still in good condition. But when they returned home in the afternoon they changed into older outfits they had worn to school the year before. These they used for doing chores, playing, and other activities at home, and they didn't discard them until they were completely worn out. The boys could be seen doing evening chores in overalls which were outgrown and had holes at the knees.

After an enjoyable session of slurping milk shakes Laura and the kids returned home. As Werner approached the car to welcome them Laura said, "Guess what, Dear. We accomplished our goal without spending more money than we budgeted."

"That's great, Honey." he replied. Then he turned to the kids and said, "Hey boys, I see you convinced your mother to buy a brand new softball. And Sarah, what's that little black thing you've got there?"

"It's my very own purse, Daddy. It has a tiny mirror too. Isn't it cute?"

Eddie chimed in and said, "Look Daddy, I got some crayons. Here, smell 'em. Don't they smell good?"

Everybody was happy. The entire shopping trip including the fifteen cent milk shakes had been a big success.

Though Eddie had to wait another year to begin kindergarten, Ron, Dale and Sarah returned to school and adapted quickly to the classroom regimen—*and* their loss of freedom! They had to admit it felt good to see all their friends and classmates again after three months of summer break.

The public elementary school was a small one-classroom building located on the corner of two gravel roads about two miles from the Schaub home. On mild weather days the kids walked both ways to and from school. At other times their parents drove them.

Although the building had electricity and also a coal furnace, plumbing was non-existent. A hand operated well provided water for a large bottle with a spigot on the bottom, which enabled the children to drain water into paper cups for drinking and into a pan for hand-washing. In the back corner of the school yard sat two outhouses which served as toilets. On each of them hung a small sign, one naturally marked "Boys" and the other "Girls".

One moonlit Halloween night a group of teen-age boys in search of excitement sneaked through a field of ripened corn to a position near those outhouses. "Now!" shouted one of the boys loudly. At the signal several boys jumped over the fence and quickly pushed both outhouses over on their sides. Just as quickly they leaped over the fence again and disappeared into the cornfield—not an unusual occurrence on Halloween but one which caused more than a little outrage in the neighborhood.

The school served also as a community center where township meetings and elections were held. In November of 1936 Werner went to the school to vote in the national presidential election. Ron accompanied him and never forgot the experience.

"Who are you voting for?" he asked.

"Franklin Roosevelt," replied his dad.

"Is he the best man?"

"Well, our nation was in bad shape from the depression four years ago when he first took office. He's helped our country a lot so I think he deserves another term."

When Roosevelt won the election by a comfortable margin, Ron believed he surely must be a great man.

A question crossed Ron's mind but he didn't say anything. He wondered why only his dad voted that day. Why didn't his mom come along and vote too? He didn't realize that women's suffrage was still relatively new and many women didn't yet exercise their right to vote, especially in rural areas.

Kathryn O'Malley was the only teacher at the school—a fine woman, older and experienced, capable and strong, fair and caring. Somehow she taught all eight elementary grades plus kindergarten in one classroom.

"I'm surprised children learn so much under these circumstances," she frequently said to the parents, "but I assure you they do."

All the parents loved Kathryn because she exercised firm discipline with just the right amount of love, understanding and encouragement—a good formula for learning. She knew how to combine classes for certain subjects, and younger students often learned a great deal just by listening to instructions being given to the older ones. Through hard work and plenty of "readin', writin' and 'rithmatic," the kids demonstrated a high level of achievement when they went to high school in the city.

Ron and his friend Tom were classmates and also excellent students. They loved to read books about sports and science and anything else that explained how things work in the universe. One day during recess the two of them approached Kathryn.

"We'd like to ask a favor," said Tom.

"Certainly, go ahead."

"Sometimes Ron and I finish our assignments before the end of the day. When that happens would it be okay if we read and studied together for a while?"

"That sounds productive and good to me. You can sit together in the hall. I do have two requests though. Would you write a very brief summary of what you learn each time, and please try not to make any noise. Is that agreeable?"

"It sure is. Thanks so much, Mrs. O'Malley!"

Dale's interests differed from Ron's and Tom's. Though only an average student at school, he excelled when it came to anything mechanical or practical. Whereas Ron thought he would rather take care of people than pigs, Dale liked taking care of pigs! He enjoyed even more helping his dad repair machinery and changing oil in the tractor.

———

Each spring eighth graders from the rural schools were required to take county achievement tests in Fort Dodge to determine if they were sufficiently prepared for high school. Generally Kathryn's students scored average or above. If a student achieved a ninety percent average or higher on the county tests, he or she was given a yellow felt letter "I", symbolizing the state of Iowa. Both Ron and Tom earned the coveted letter and proudly asked their mothers to sew it on one of their shirts. Five years later little Eddie, who wasn't so little anymore, matched the achievement of his older brother.

Everyone looked forward to recess. The teacher got a break and the kids got a chance to let off steam. When pleasant weather prevailed the girls might join the boys in a game of softball or kickball. But often they simply walked around the play ground and talked about everything under the sun, including the boys of course!

As for the boys, they wanted to expend energy and have fun. With only one teacher on duty and little supervision, their games sometimes became rough and even dangerous.

One day a sixth grade boy named Alvin had a good idea, or so he thought. He approached his father and asked, "Do you need that old front tractor tire leaning against the garage?"

"I don't think so. Why?" asked his father.

"I'd like to take it to school?"

"What for?"

"Just to roll it around the playground during recess, maybe play some games with it."

"I guess it would be okay if you don't do anything foolish."

During the noon break the next day the boys had a good time playing with the tire, rolling it at each other and also at the girls. By the second day they were looking for something more exciting to do with the tire. One of them suggested they take it over to the gravel road which had a slight downward grade. There they began a new game which was a little scary. One boy curled his body inside the tire while two others rolled it down the road at a moderate speed, running beside and steadying it. That was truly fun and exciting!

After a few boys took turns Dale said, "I'd like to give it a try if it's okay with you guys." He was a second grader and younger than most of the other boys, but daring and enthusiastic. Also he was tall and strong for his age.

"Sure Dale, climb in," replied Eric, a sixth grader who had a sadistic tendency.

Eric decided to give Dale the ride of his life. After getting the tire rolling as fast as he could run, Eric suddenly stopped and abandoned it! Poor Dale rolled helplessly out of control, round and around. Finally both tire and passenger lost balance and crashed into the ditch beside the road. Dale escaped serious injury but suffered a sprained wrist and a nasty bruise on one leg. Restraining a tear, he limped over to Eric and pushed him to the ground with all his might. Eric jumped back up but considered it the better part of wisdom not to retaliate. He was concerned about what Kathryn would say and do.

When she heard what happened Kathryn raced to the scene carrying her first aid kit. After treating Dale's wounds as best she could she announced, "Students, please go to the classroom. I want to have a talk with you."

She was *very* unhappy not only with Eric but also herself. From the beginning she thought she should have banned the tire from school. When the students were settled at their desks she gazed at them with a look that was both stern and forgiving.

"I have only three things I want to say to you," she began. "First, the tire goes home today after school and does not come back. Second, any unusual 'toys' must not be brought to school unless I approve them first, *especially* if they could be dangerous. And third, I respect every one of you but I want you to use common sense."

Kathryn suspended Eric for the rest of the week because his offense was intentional.

―⊷∞⊶―

The next school year Eddie began kindergarten and immediately fell in "puppy love" with Judy, one of his classmates. They received the brunt of much teasing and giggling but that didn't bother them. For a while they walked home together hand in hand after school. Although the romance ended as quickly as it began, the two young students continued their friendship and even skipped a grade together. Under Kathryn's guidance they breezed through the third and fourth grades in one year. Eddie was comfortable and friendly with people of all ages. He liked school and had many friends.

———

Each year the enrollment at the school decreased as students migrated to parochial church schools in order to receive religious instruction along with the other subjects. One spring day as Ron was nearing the end of sixth grade, Laura and Werner entered the classroom after school to speak with Kathryn.

"We're sorry to tell you this," Laura said sadly, "but we want you to know that next fall we'll be transferring Ron to our church's school so he can be part of the confirmation program."

"I certainly understand and I appreciate your telling me early," Kathryn replied.

"We hate to do it," added Werner, "but we feel it's important for Ron."

"If I were in your shoes I'd probably do the same thing."

"May I add something?" said Laura. "We know that Ron and our other kids will not get a better education than they've received here. You've done a magnificent job. It's just that we want them to have religious instruction."

"Thanks for the compliment," said Kathryn. "I'm sure you know I've enjoyed working with all your children. Believe me, I'll truly miss Ron."

A few years later the little public school on the corner had so few students it had to be closed. The remaining children who had not transferred elsewhere were bused to a consolidated school in a town several miles away. Thereafter the tiny white building deteriorated quickly. Paint on the outside walls peeled; a few shingles blew away; grass grew tall and was seldom cut; everything looked unkempt. In the end the township used the building only for an occasional meeting—and for stirring up cherished memories in those who drove by in their car.

4. Harvest Moon

As October drew near the harvest moon rose rose brilliantly on the eastern horizon. One evening Werner and Laura sat on metal chairs in the front yard enjoying the beautiful bright ball in the sky.

"The moon is unusually orange tonight," said Werner.

"Yes, it's gorgeous," Laura replied. "And notice how big it looks."

"Ron says the moon always looks bigger when it's near the horizon and shines through the atmosphere. With all his reading about space he's turning into quite an astronomer."

"I think that's great...Wanna go inside? I'm starting to feel cold."

"Yup, I think it's time."

They had also noticed the sun sinking in the west about a minute earlier each evening, taking along its warmth and leaving behind a chill in the air. Somehow the corn seemed to understand these signs of nature and turned more brown and dry each passing day. The time for harvest was near at hand.

The summer of 1935 had provided plenty of rain and sunshine until early August when suddenly it turned hot and dry. By that time the corn had already reached sufficient maturity so that the harvest promised to be a bountiful one. This reassured Werner since the payments on his recently purchased land were due to begin the following March.

"If we can fill our crib this fall," he said to Laura, "we'll be able to handle those payments next year without a problem."

Werner and his neighbor George worked together at harvest time. Some tasks required more than one person such as hoisting and bolting the corn harvester to the frame of a tractor. Together George and Werner accomplished it without difficulty.

"Shall we give it a try?" asked Werner.

"Absolutely," replied George.

Werner climbed to the seat of the tractor and engaged the gears. A loud roaring noise ensued but everything seemed to work okay. Werner was so surrounded by the harvester components that only his head could be seen. Sitting in the midst of such an operating machine while driving it down the corn rows involved some risk. More than a few farmers lost fingers and even arms trying to reach and dislodge a corn stalk that had become stuck in the revolving rollers without stopping the machinery first.

The McDonalds and Schaubs understood that teamwork was essential. One farmer picked the corn in the field while another emptied a full wagon back home. A power driven elevator carried the corn to the top of the crib roof and dropped it inside through an opening.

Since the crib stood just sixty feet west of the house it was easy for the kids to watch this activity from the kitchen window.

Meanwhile a third person used a tractor to pull wagons back and forth between the field and the crib. Laura and Betty McDonald, George's wife, frequently volunteered for this job because of a shortage of workers and because they liked to drive the tractor. Certainly it was more fun than using horses as they did in earlier years. That required hitching and unhitching a team of horses to a wagon many times each day—*not* fun.

Laura had several roles to fill—prepare meals, transport children to and from school, help with the harvest, and see that the evening chores were done. Being a strong woman like her mother, she could keep up with most men when it came to hard work. The kids helped when they arrived home from school by regularly doing many of the evening chores such as watering and feeding the animals.

It took only a few days to complete the corn picking at the Schaub farm. Immediately George and Werner began moving the equipment to George's fields which were less than a mile down the road. Since it was Saturday with no school, Tom and Ron were hoping they could help.

Werner approached them and said, "Would you guys like to pull a wagon over to McDonalds with one of the tractors?"

"Sure!" they shouted enthusiastically.

Neither was quite ten years old, but nine seemed to be the accepted age at which farm boys began driving a tractor. Poor Dale felt jealous. Because he had just turned seven he and their dog Rex had to be satisfied with riding along inside the wagon. Ron and Tom felt proud and thrilled that they were able to participate in "men's work."

They continued the same process of corn picking at George's farm. However on the very first day an accident stopped everything for a few hours. Inside the crib a ladder ascended to the top of the bins. Tom, Ron and Dale thought it would be interesting to climb to the top of the ladder and watch the corn pouring in from above. As they climbed upward Ron followed directly behind Dale. About half way up Dale's foot slipped and he stepped back one rung on the ladder to regain his balance. Ron had already grasped that rung and Dale's foot came down heavily on his hand. Surprised and shocked, Ron pulled his hand away and fell off the ladder.

Fortunately he hit soft dirt at the bottom, but on the way down his head struck the wheel of a wagon parked in the crib. The other two boys hurried down and helped him to his feet.

"I think I'm okay," said Ron.

"No, you're not!" cried Tom as he caught sight of a tiny stream of blood spurting outward a few inches from the back of Ron's head.

The boys led him to the house where George's wife Betty met them. She ran inside and grabbed a clean white towel which she wrapped tightly around Ron's head.

"What happened?" shouted Werner and George as they came running toward the house. There wasn't time to do much explaining.

"Ron has a nasty cut on his head," said Betty. "I think he should be seen by a doctor as soon as possible. The clinic in Webster City is open until two o'clock on Saturdays."

George jumped into the driver's seat of his car as Werner helped Ron into the back seat. The three of them sped down the road in a cloud of dust and quickly disappeared from sight.

"He'll probably be all right; his thinking and his speech were clear," said Betty as she tried to comfort the other boys. Tom felt deep concern about his friend. Dale suffered guilt because it was his foot which caused Ron to lose his grip on the ladder. Betty phoned Laura and told her what happened. Obviously shaken by the news, Laura put Sarah and Eddie in the car and quickly drove to McDonalds.

About two hours later George and his passengers arrived back home. Ron exited from the back seat with a white bandage around his head. Everyone rushed to his side and gave him a hug.

"Are you all right, Ronnie?" asked Laura, hoping for a positive response.

"Sure," he replied. "I just got a little bump and cut on my head."

"I wouldn't call it little since several stitches were needed," stated Werner. "The doctor said he'd like to see Ron again in about a week to remove the stitches. He hopes Ron will be okay by then."

Relief appeared on the faces of everyone, especially Dale and Tom.

"I'm really sorry," said Dale.

"Don't worry, accidents happen," said Ron. "I shouldn't have been so close behind you on that crazy ladder." Such confession and forgiveness were hardlytypical among the kids.

Werner gave Ron a second hug and said, "I'm sorry too. I should have known where you guys were, but I didn't. I hope you know how important you are to us."

He came close to saying he loved Ron but he couldn't quite get the words out. Werner loved his children very much but found it difficult to say so. Having been raised in a family that rarely expressed feelings and emotions made it hard for him to be demonstrative. Seldom did he hug even Laura except when the kids were not around.

Laura made up for Werner's deficiency by frequently expressing her love for the children. Perhaps the only person she should have loved more was herself, which may have stemmed from her early childhood with Grandma Bauer.

She demonstrated this trait by regularly urging people not to go out of their way for her, as if she didn't deserve it. Yet she would always be ready to go out of *her* way for others, especially the children. She's the one who provided the kids with the love they needed. They felt it every night when she tucked them into bed with the endearing words: "Goodnight my little sweet potatoes."

However Laura's love did not keep her from being a firm disciplinarian. Her children took her seriously when she threatened a spanking because they feared her tool of choice—a fifteen inch piece of rubber hose. How it did sting! One day Eddie told Dale he was going to get rid of that horrible hose.

"How?" asked Dale.

"I'm going to take it into the cornfield and throw it as far as I can."

"Sounds good. I admire your courage."

Eddie carried out his plan, but to his chagrin an identical hose soon appeared in Laura's broom closet.

———

A couple days later the crew finished picking corn at George's farm. Immediately they removed the harvester from the tractor and returned it to the storage shed.

That evening Werner said to Laura, "I'm happy with the corn yield we got. Now I feel better about our land purchase."

"Didn't I say we needed to have a little faith?" replied Laura.

Pretending to ignore her question Werner continued, "With the added acreage I'm going to need more help next year. I've been thinking about hiring a young man who could stay with us—maybe someone like Norm Johnson's oldest son, Steve. How would you feel about that?"

After a short pause Laura said, "Sounds okay but I must admit I'm a little uneasy about bringing Steve into our family circle."

"Why is that?"

"It would change our family dynamics. Also there's much we don't know about Steve. For example why did he drop out of high school last winter in the middle of his junior year?"

"Lots of young people drop out of high school. I think he'd get along well with the boys because they like him. He's a strong good looking teen-ager who's not afraid of hard work."

"Well," mused Laura, "I suppose we could try it for one summer and see how it works before we make a final decision."

"Good idea! I'll have a talk with Steve and his dad tomorrow."

The meeting went well and the Johnson's liked the proposal. Steve seemed glad for the opportunity to earn money and Norm felt good about his son expending energy in a healthy way. It was agreed that Steve would begin his new job in March of the following year; would receive room and board in addition to a salary; and would share the benefits *and* responsibilities of a family member. On Saturday evenings and Sundays he would return home and spend time with his own family. Everyone seemed pleased with the arrangement.

Filled with excitement the Schaub boys looked forward to having a handsome, muscular young man living with them.

"It'll be almost like having an older brother," said Dale.

Though hesitant to express her misgivings Laura kept asking herself, *"To what extent will Steve be a role model for the boys—good or bad?"* Seeking reassurance she recalled that the first year would be only a trial.

───

As winter approached Werner announced to the boys, "I think we should start getting our house ready for cold weather."

"Using straw again?" asked Dale.

"Yup. We'll pile a layer of straw over the basement windows and the foundation. That should provide a little insulation."

"Won't the wind blow some of it away?"

"We'll try to keep that from happening by covering the straw with some thin wire fence."

When baling became common a few years later Werner used heavy straw bales instead of loose straw.

Keeping the home warm in the winter proved to be a challenge. The Schaubs didn't have a furnace in the basement, just a coal burning stove in the dining room and a small cooking stove fueled with corn cobs in the kitchen. Both of these vented into a chimney which was in the center of the house. When the family came inside from the cold they often gathered around the stove in the dining room, placing their nearly frozen feet close to the heat. What a pleasant comfortable feeling!

Metal registers in the ceilings allowed a little heat to rise into the bedrooms upstairs but they remained cold nonetheless. After the stoves burned out during the night the bedrooms became frigid. However this didn't keep the family from being cozy and warm as they slept, thanks to blankets filled with down and feathers from last summer's crop of geese. Getting up in the morning was another matter. The bedrooms were so cold the kids could see their breath and the window panes so covered with frost they could hardly see anything outside.

Snuggled in their warm feather bed the boys often talked for a while before going to sleep, sometimes in mid-sentence. One night Dale confidently announced, "I'm going to earn a million dollars before I'm forty years old."

"Sure you are," responded Ron with disgust. "Just like I'm going to live to be a hundred! You don't know what you're talking about."

Meanwhile Eddie who slept in the opposite corner of the room regularly said the evening prayer he learned from his mother:

"Now I lay me down to sleep, I pray the Lord my soul to keep.
If I should die before I wake, I pray the Lord my soul to take."

Years later publishers changed the last line of the prayer to something more appropriate for five year olds:

"Thy love be with me through the night, and wake me with the morning light."

To preserve heat during the winter Laura closed the door leading into the living room.

"It's ironic that the most comfortable and well furnished room in the house is too cold to use all winter long," she thought.

She made one exception. Whenever she expected company she opened the door in advance to make the room warm and welcoming for the guests.

Werner signed up for electricity as soon as it became available. In the 1930's many rural Iowans finally got electricity connected to their homes and barns, thanks to the Rural Electrification Act approved by the Federal Government as part of the New Deal. This brought about significant changes in lifestyle for all the farmers.

Now Laura could store perishable food in a refrigerator instead of the icebox. Everyone could play table games or read at any time of the day or night. When extremely cold outside Werner placed an electric heater in the barn, enabling sows and their newborn litters to sleep comfortably without danger of freezing to death.

"I'm glad we finally have a radio," said Sarah. "I like to listen to funny guys like Jack Benny and Red Skelton."

The boys and their dad found it exciting to gather around the large box radio and listen to a blow by blow broadcast of a championship boxing match between Joe Louis and one of his outclassed opponents.

One important change was still missing: running water. A fifty foot high windmill filled a tank for the livestock while a hand-pumped well provided fresh water for the house. Laura kept a pail on the kitchen counter from which the family scooped water with a ladle for drinking, cooking and hand washing. Because they didn't have a bathroom in the home, an outhouse in the back yard served as a toilet—a chilling experience in the winter. When it was extremely cold a portable toilet in the basement served as a substitute.

Every Saturday night the three boys took baths in a round metal tub half filled with warm water, taking turns getting into the tub first. Since the last boy had to bathe in water that was neither warm nor clean, controversy often erupted over whose turn it was to be first. Sarah turned out to be the lucky one. She didn't need to compete with anyone and always had perfect water.

Werner noticed the long hard winter passing and the snow beginning to melt. Soon the 1936 cycle of farming would begin, except this time around it would be different. There would be more of everything—more land (240 acres instead of 160), more work, more costs, more debt, and hopefully more profit. He had high hopes but also a little apprehension.

5. Black Dust

"It always feels great when we start seeding oats," said Werner happily. "It's a sure sign spring has arrived even if it's still cold outside." It was the spring of 1936.

"I know, I feel the same way," agreed Laura.

Steve Johnson, now a strong seventeen year old, arrived for work at the beginning of March as had been agreed. Werner assigned him part of the daily chores and introduced him to the operation of the farm machinery. Both got off to a good start working together on the oats seeding. Steve shredded the previous season's corn stalks and loosened the soil with a tractor and disc. Werner followed with a team of horses, a wagon of oats, and a spreader on the back of the wagon which hurled the seeds about twenty feet in every direction. Steve finished up with the tractor and harrow, smoothing the soil and burying the seeds. In just two days they completed the job.

That evening Werner said to Laura, "I'm happy with Steve so far. He's doing a good job."

"Glad to hear it; let's hope it continues," replied Laura.

For some reason which she herself could not fully understand, Laura still felt uneasy about Steve. Yet, his initial impression on every other member of the family seemed positive. The boys were impressed by the size of his biceps and his willingness to "fool around." Sarah summarized her feelings very briefly: With a grin she said, "I think he's really cute."

"What's next?" asked Steve.

"Shelling last fall's corn crop," answered Werner. "But it won't be difficult because I've hired a sheller who owns all the equipment. I've also lined up two truckers to haul the corn to the grain elevator in town. Should only take a day and a half."

Schaub's dog Rex enjoyed shelling more than anyone. As the men extracted corn from one end of the crib, rats and mice which had made their homes in the husks gradually moved to the other end. When only a small amount of corn remained, the rodents began leaping to the ground through air gaps in the crib siding. Rex ran back and forth with much excitement, catching as many as possible in his jaw while they were still in midair. One quick snap of his powerful head and the poor rodent was history. He wanted to help and in a way he did. At least Rex had great fun that day! In retrospect it seems cruel but farmers considered rodents the enemy. After all, they ate and destroyed a lot of grain.

When they finished shelling Steve asked, "What are we going to do with that huge pile of cobs?"

"Later we'll load them into the spreader and scatter them in the fields," Werner replied. "Over the winter they'll rot and become fertilizer."

A funny thing happened to Steve one day while he was shoveling cobs into the spreader—funny to an observer but not to Steve. Looking for a place to hide, a mouse ran through the husks and scurried up one of Steve's pant legs. Frantically he pulled off his pants and shook them vigorously! Now clad only in a straw hat and white jockey shorts, Steve hoped against hope that Laura and Sarah were not watching from the house!

It nearly turned out that Steve wouldn't *need* to haul any more cobs to the field. A week after the shelling Sarah and Eddie played house near the edge of the pile. Using cobs to build make-believe rooms, they placed a wood box in the center to serve as a table. Sarah brought a candle from the house and placed it on the table.

"I'll light the candle," said Eddie who just happened to have a book of matches in his pocket.

"Be careful with those matches!" warned Sarah.

Shortly after he lit the candle a gust of wind blew it over and it rolled into a stack of dry husks. Immediately a fire ignited and spread rapidly.

"I told you to be careful," shouted Sarah as she ran toward the house to alert her mother.

Surprised and frightened, Eddie didn't know what to do or say.

Werner came running from the barn which was only a short distance north of the crib. He could see that the fire was already too large for him to put out by himself. Laura burst out of the house just in time to hear him shout, "Call the fire department quick! We need help!"

When Laura dialed the operator half the neighbors picked up their receivers on the party line and listened to her pleas for help. Soon the whole community knew about the emergency. A short time later a fire truck arrived with a large tank full of water. Behind it followed a line of cars filled with helpful neighbors who had brought buckets, shovels, five gallon milk cans filled with water, and anything else they thought might help.

For a while the situation looked bad as the flames shot up to the roof of the crib and set a few shingles on fire. Many, including Werner, feared the worst. The truck aimed one of its water hoses at the crib and the other at the burning cobs, while the neighbors flung as many buckets of water on the flames as they could muster. With the combined efforts of everyone the fire was subdued and finally extinguished. Laura and Werner expressed relief and their deepest gratitude to all who helped. Later that evening they remembered to give sincere thanks to God as well.

A neighbor remarked, "I never realized listening in on a party line could do so much good!" Everyone laughed knowingly.

But where was Eddie? No one had seen him since the fire started. After a long and extensive search they finally found him sobbing in the closet of the boys' upstairs bedroom. He knew he had made a dangerous mistake and feared the punishment which he assumed would surely come. However good fortune was with him that day. Instead of punishment he got only compassion and consolation. All were relieved and happy to find him safe. And everyone, especially his parents, became much more cautious about their children using matches. A lesson well learned!

<hr />

Early one morning Werner said to Laura, "Hey, Honey, how about a date?"

"Got anything in mind?" she answered with an incredulous but playful smile.

"Well, I know you want to do some shopping and I'd like to go to the bank and make a mortgage payment with the money we got from the corn. I thought we might splurge a bit and have lunch together. Then while you're shopping I'll go to the implement dealer and look at some farm equipment."

Laura couldn't hold back a chuckle. "I *thought* you might have something more in mind than just a date for the two of us."

"Okay, okay, you caught me," said Werner laughing. "But with a bigger farm and a hired worker we know we're going to need more machinery," he countered.

Both had a good time in town and each accomplished what they hoped to do. However Werner's extravagance exceeded his own intentions. He made a down payment not only on a hay loader but also on a used tractor. Unlike the tractor he already owned, this one had thick steel blades on the back wheels instead of tires. Blades were great for traction but not for a smooth ride on hard surfaces such as gravel roads.

"Can we afford all that?" asked Laura.

"I'll have to make time payments," replied Werner. "With bigger crops we should be okay."

"I wish you would discuss such large purchases with me first."

"You weren't there and I didn't want to risk losing the chance to buy the machinery at such a good price."

"But what if we had a crop failure? How would we make payments then? We'd really be in a pickle! Shouldn't we at least discuss such possibilities before we leap?"

"I guess you're right, Honey. I'll remember that next time."

Though quite upset Laura dropped the matter, hoping Werner would keep his pledge to do things differently in the future.

When the machinery arrived Werner eagerly tested the tractor during corn planting and was pleased with it. Steve again prepared the plowed fields with the disc and harrow while Werner followed with a two-row corn planter.

Beginning that year the farming operations required more time because they had to be done both at home and at the 80 acre site. Transporting the machinery back and forth also took additional time, especially when using the tractor with the bladed wheels.

Two days after the completion of corn planting a refreshing shower of rain fell on the fields. It seemed almost providential. The kernels germinated quickly and soon tiny plants of corn popped up through the soil. For Werner that was a beautiful sight to behold.

"Just look at all those little green rows stretching across the field," he said to his family joyfully. "It certainly is a miracle!"

Unfortunately that was the last rain that fell for a number of weeks. Werner's excitement gave way to concern as the weather became unseasonably hot and dry. Trying to look on the bright side he said, "At least the oats is mature enough to make a good crop. It looks great."

When the oats was bright yellow Werner said to Ron, "Do you think you're ready to drive the tractor and binder?"

"You bet I am," said Ron, thrilled at the prospect. Dale was less thrilled because he believed he could drive just as well as Ron in spite of being two years younger.

It was a busy time. While Steve cultivated the corn Ron and Werner cut the oats. Sitting on the binder, Werner dropped groups of four or five bundles in straight rows across the field. Later he and his crew of Steve and the two boys would manually place all the bundles into shocks so the grain would dry. Shocking was a hot, sticky and tedious job.

As he and his dad were cutting oats Ron noticed something that troubled him. Sometimes his dad seemed careless when working hard. An example of this occurred when a dry corn stalk from the previous year got stuck in the sickle bar of the binder. Werner whistled loudly as a signal to stop. Ron stepped on the clutch stopping both the tractor and the power drive to the binder. Werner then climbed down from his seat, knelt in front of the sickle bar and dislodged the obstruction.

Ron sensed that if his foot were to slip off the clutch his father might be seriously injured or even killed. Quickly he disengaged the gears and the power drive. Thereafter he continued to do the same each time Werner prepared to crawl in front of the binder. Ron often questioned in his mind why his dad had not cautioned him about this risky situation from the very beginning. "*Was it because he moved fast and failed to consider the danger?"* Ron wondered. *"It's a good thing Mom didn't see all of this. She would have been really upset."*

On the farm danger always hovered on the edges. Eddie possibly came closer to a fatal accident than anyone else in the family. One summer afternoon he asked Steve if he could ride along on the tractor, the one with the bladed wheels. Steve agreed—hardly a wise decision since Eddie was just six. As they crossed a plowed field Eddie stood on the platform of the right rear axle and held on to the fender. Temporarily releasing his grasp he pointed his finger at a large cloud in the sky and asked Steve, "How long do you think it would take to climb a ladder that reached from the ground to that cloud?"

Before Steve could answer the front wheels of the tractor dropped into a hole, apparently dug by a wild animal. Immediately the tractor stopped. Eddie, his arm still pointing to the sky, fell to the ground in front of the right wheel. One of its steel blades came down on his shoulder but then stopped abruptly. The left wheel continued spinning, its sharp blades digging fiercely into the dirt. All of this happened so fast Eddie hardly had time to be frightened, but of course it shocked him. He suffered a cut and bruise on his shoulder but miraculously no critical injuries. His family and the neighbors shuddered when they considered what could have happened if the wheel on his shoulder had also kept spinning.

The shoulder healed but a serious question remained: why did one wheel remain motionless while the other did not? Some were convinced it was a miracle, a gift from God. Terribly shaken, Laura accepted that premise.

After much discussion Werner and Steve arrived at a theory which they considered likely. The tractor had a double brake, they explained, one for each back wheel. The driver could push both together for full braking or he could push just one when turning sharply. In a split second Steve tried desperately to hit the clutch with his left foot and the double brake with his right. Apparently in his haste he missed all except the right brake. This left the tractor in gear, the right wheel motionless, and the left wheel spinning.

Whether that's truly what happened will never be known with certainty.

Steve apologized several times for any responsibility he may have had in the accident, but no one blamed him. On the contrary the family thanked him effusively for his quick response which may have saved Eddie's life.

"I do think we should agree on something however," stated Laura. "In the future no one under the age of nine should ride on a tractor which is at work in the fields."

Werner and Steve concurred.

That night everyone in the family offered thanksgiving to God and love to one another.

—❧—

Two days later the telephone rang. "Hi Werner, this is Lloyd Olson," said the voice on the other end. "Do you think your oats shocks are dry enough for threshing? We should begin as soon as possible before it rains."

"To tell you the truth I wish it would rain," replied Werner, "but yes, my shocks are ready. When can we start?"

"I'll move the thresher to your place tomorrow and we can start the next day."

Lloyd owned a large threshing machine which he powered with a huge turn-of-the-century steam engine tractor. He was a skilled mechanic who loved to keep his old machinery operating almost forever. Usually all he needed was an oil can, a wrench and a screw driver. Each year in early July he moved his tractor and thresher from one farm to another in what they called a "threshing run." His only responsibility was to keep the machinery running smoothly.

Several farmers and their sons joined together in this major effort with each having a specific job. One group went to the fields with their horses, hayracks, and forks and brought back big loads of bundles. Each pitched his bundles into the thresher one by one, a very strenuous activity. Thinking it would be fun and challenging, Tom and Ron offered to unload one of the racks. However they found the work more difficult than imagined and became thoroughly exhausted by the time the rack was half empty. A little embarrassed, they gave up!

Nevertheless the boys took turns fulfilling a different responsibility, a much easier one. They helped load the wagon boxes by pushing the oats to the front and back with a shovel. Because a cloud of dust surrounded them as they worked, the boys found their job somewhat unpleasant. Still, they were proud to be part of the team. Steve and two other men hauled the wagons back and forth to the crib, emptying the oats into the bins via the elevator.

Perhaps the most difficult task belonged to the man who stood on top of the thresher and guided the straw blower, creating a rounded semi-waterproof straw pile. Werner and another farmer took turns doing that job. Dust surrounded them all day and by evening they were hardly recognizable. On evening Werner came walking toward the house covered with dust.

"You look like a black man!" Dale joked.

"Maybe I am," replied Werner smiling, his sparkling white teeth standing out in sharp contrast.

Although threshing was hard work everyone looked forward to it. The men enjoyed talking, joking, and working together. The kids creatively mixed work and play. The women loved bringing their favorite potluck dishes which they served on a large table under a tree in the yard. Under the same tree Sarah happily filled and refilled two pans with cool water which the workers appreciated when they washed their hands and sweaty faces. All who sat around the table shared conversation, laughter and a wonderful meal. It was a communal event which gave everyone, both young and old, a sense of cooperation and accomplishment. As the sun set slowly at the end of a long day, neighbors felt bonded in a community of interdependence.

"I think we set a record this year," stated Lloyd after completing the threshing run at all four participating farms. "Since it didn't rain we finished in just two weeks!"

"What's even more remarkable, the harvest was good considering the small amount of rain we got," added George.

Later Laura said to Werner, "I hear the oats did okay."

"Yup. Probably the spring rains helped. That's good because we got enough oats to feed the animals and still have some left to sell."

"Will that see us through?"

"I'm afraid not. We'll still be in trouble if the corn doesn't get rain soon. The leaves are curling and turning brown and the soil is so dry that the wind is starting to blow some of it away."

"It seems everyone's praying for rain," said Laura.

"We need that. Today's newspaper reported severe dust storms in a number of western states. We certainly don't want that here."

"I wish we had some good news."

"Wait a minute, Honey, there is *some* good news. Do you remember, after we sold our corn I used part of the money to pay a couple months ahead on the mortgage."

"Thank goodness for that! It gives us a little space to breathe."

"Let's not worry too much," Werner concluded. "Who knows? It may rain tonight."

It didn't rain that night, nor any night for another several weeks. Instead it became unusually hot and dry. On windy days waves of dust whipped through the fields and into the sky, further stressing the corn and setting the farmers' nerves on edge. The summer of 1936 would long be remembered.

Day after day the temperature hovered near one hundred degrees in the daytime and about ninety at night. The heat was relentless. Because the Schaubs' bedrooms were uncomfortably hot at bedtime, they started taking sheets and pillows to the yard at night and lying on the grass for a while. Unexpected benefits came from this practice as everyone began to describe experiences, tell stories and share feelings. A sense of closeness enveloped the family as the problems of heat and drought temporarily faded from their consciousness.

One evening when they were lying on the grass and gazing into the sky Sarah said, "Look how big and bright the moon is. Why is it so much bigger than the stars?"

"It isn't bigger, just much closer," replied her mother.

"Look at that bright star just below the moon!" exclaimed Dale.

Ron the "astronomer" responded, "That's not a star. That's the planet Jupiter. It goes around the sun just like the earth does. It's bright because it's so huge."

Unconsciously they were meditating on the immensity of the universe and soon began to experience a sense of awe in the presence of God. Often they found it difficult to pick themselves up from the grassy beds and head back to their hot bedrooms.

Finally near the end of July a light shower of rain descended on the parched corn fields. "Hooray!" shouted Werner gleefully. "That will help, but we need much more."

Throughout August very little rain fell, just a few sprinkles. Much of the corn dried on the cob unable to mature.

After the fall harvest Werner reported the bad news to Laura. "It appears the forecasters were right. This year's corn yield is only about fifty percent of average. Not a very good first year on our own larger farm. I'm afraid we're facing some difficult days ahead, financially speaking."

"That's not good of course," she responded, "but we can't give up. I believe we'll make it somehow."

"I hope you're right. If so it'll be by the grace of God."

The following year of 1937 was even worse. Very little rain fell throughout the spring and summer. The unrelenting heat and drought combined with immense dust storms in the western plains made that an unforgettable year. Fortunately Iowa was not hit by dust as severely as some other states. Nevertheless Werner, George and their neighbors did everything possible to stop the dust from rolling, such as cultivating more frequently and sowing oats or alfalfa on loose soil. Yet their crops suffered major damage.

The situation became even more disastrous in states such as Texas, Oklahoma, and Kansas where strong winds lifted dust aloft, causing so-called black rollers or black blizzards. Layers of dust settled inside of homes on window sills, tables, beds—everywhere! Outside their homes people found dust banks piled as high as three feet. The resulting darkness led chickens roosting in their coops to fall asleep thinking it was night.

One Sunday in April in the mid-1930s the atmosphere was so darkened it was called Black Sunday. The blackness rose in the sky and was carried by upper winds all the way to the Atlantic Ocean. When people living in Washington D.C. and New York City looked upward, they were able to see dark clouds in the distance. Farm analysts and newspapers agreed that the dust storms of the 1930's were an ecological and agricultural disaster, not to mention the human cost. According to some estimates one hundred million acres of land had been rendered barren.

George and Tom invited Werner and his boys to an exploratory walk through one of their corn fields. It didn't present a pretty picture. The corn plants were brown with small ears and very few kernels.

"It looks awful. Why does this happen?" Tom asked.

"Farming is unpredictable," replied George. "Most years are good, thank God, but occasionally a few are not. I guess we have to look at the big picture."

"What does that mean?"

"We're grateful for the good years and we try to take the bad years in stride. In the long run we usually come out ahead."

"But what if this happens again next year?" demanded Dale.

"The Farm Associations are making helpful suggestions," replied George. "One of the most obvious is crop rotation."

"We're already doing that, aren't we we Dad?" observed Ron.

"Yes," said Werner. "We plant corn or soy beans in a field one year and oats the next. In that way we expose the loose soil to the wind only every *other* year. Another good idea is strip farming."

"What's that?"

"It's planting strips of various crops next to each other, such as first a strip of corn, next a strip of oats, then one of soy beans, maybe a strip of alfalfa hay, and so on. That prevents the wind and dust from building momentum and beginning to roll."

"Strip farming sounds like fun," said Eddie.

"Another good idea," added George, "is that we should not plow under any of our grassy pastures to convert them into row crops. Instead they suggest we keep the pastures in grass and use them to raise a few more cattle."

At least one positive thing came out of the dust storms. Very quickly farmers became conscious of the need for soil conservation. The agriculture department at Iowa State University in Ames intensified its research and, together with the State Department of Agriculture, suggested new methods of conservation each year. Over the decades this improved the way farming was done.

The dust and drought presented Laura and Werner with financial concerns as the pressure of their land mortgage began to weigh heavily on them.

"When does that advance payment you made to the bank run out, Dear?" asked Laura.

"Next month," said Werner. "I don't know what we'll do after that. It's obvious we won't get much of a corn crop this fall. Forecasters are estimating this year's yield will be only twenty percent of normal. Frankly Honey, we're against the wall."

"Don't say anything to the kids. I don't want them to worry."

"Right, good idea."

After a brief pause Laura continued, "I hate to suggest this but maybe I could ask my parents for another loan."

"No, I'd rather not do that. I feel too indebted to them already! George told me the bank gave him a brief extension on his loan in view of the extreme weather. I'll talk to the bank tomorrow and see if they'll do the same for us."

Next day the bank's loan officer said to Werner, "Yes, we'll give you the extension. But I must caution you that we'll expect a full repayment of the mortgage plus extra interest for the extension."

"I understand," replied Werner. "Though it's a struggle right now we're determined to pay our debt in full."

"Great," said the banker. "What about your land taxes? Will you be able to pay them?"

"I think so, but frankly I don't know how just yet."

"Okay, good luck."

Later Werner shared with Laura the good news about the bank extension and both felt a sense of relief.

"I've always said there's good news behind the bad," exclaimed Laura.

"Let me add one more good thing," said Werner. "We'll always be able to eat, thanks to the garden and the animals."

The Schaubs had a large garden which provided an ample supply of fruits and vegetables. It was fun when everyone worked together in the garden. Periodically a man from town with a small truck came to their home and purchased eggs and cream which they had garnered from their chickens and cows. Money from those sales paid for groceries and other necessities. Occasionally they butchered a few young chickens to provide fresh meat for the table.

Everyone considered it a special treat when sweet corn was picked fresh from the field, cooked immediately, and placed on the table while still steaming hot. Add a little butter and it was a super treat! The availability of fresh homegrown food was indeed a blessing.

That evening after supper Eddie approached Laura with a tear in his eye and exclaimed, "Boy am I mad!"

"What's wrong, sweetheart?" she asked.

"Somebody broke my bank and all my money is gone."

He handed his mother a small metal bank shaped like a baseball on a stand. On top of the ball a narrow slit allowed coins to be dropped inside. A round cap on the bottom could be opened with a key. This time however the cap had been pried off with a powerful tool, like a screwdriver or knife perhaps. Not surprisingly the broken bank contained nothing.

"Who would do such a thing?" Laura demanded.

The family discussed many possibilities. Eventually Steve's name came up.

"Yesterday Steve and I stopped in Homer to pick up a few groceries," stated Werner. "While I paid the cashier I noticed Steve at the other end of the counter buying a package of cigarettes. I thought that was rather strange because I've never seen Steve smoke and he rarely carries money in his pocket."

"I wonder if his parents know he smokes," said Laura.

After much consideration they decided they should ask Steve if he knew anything about Eddie's broken bank.

At first Steve denied any knowledge of what happened. However after a brief discussion he remorsefully confessed that he had pilfered Eddie's bank.

"I don't know why I did it," he said. "I guess I was trying to keep up with a few of my friends and I needed some change to buy cigarettes."

"But why would you do this to Eddie?" asked Laura.

"I feel really bad about Eddie. I swear I'll buy him a new bank and pay back every nickel I took."

"We appreciate your taking responsibility," replied Werner, "but I'm afraid we'll have to share this with your parents."

"I hope I can keep on working here," said Steve with a worried expression on his face.

"You've done a good job for us, Steve. No complaints on that score. Still, Laura and I need to talk with your parents and see how they feel. You don't need to go along."

As expected Norm and Claire Johnson were upset when they heard what Steve had done. Norm's first inclination was to bring him home and discipline him in some way. As the discussion continued, though, opinions began to change. In the end all agreed that since Steve had worked so faithfully he should be given a second chance. That would give him the opportunity to develop responsibility, save money, and perhaps even consider finishing high school. Of course he would need to prove himself.

Steve felt immensely relieved when told about the decision. Werner said, "We've agreed with your parents that you can continue working for us this summer and at least one more season next year. Is that okay with you?"

"Sure, that would be great," Steve answered enthusiastically.

The solution made everyone in the family happy because they had grown fond of Steve.

———

The next day Werner and the boys were cleaning the barn, shoveling manure into the spreader and replacing it with clean straw. Suddenly Laura came running and exclaimed, "Hey Honey, my dad's on the phone; he wants to talk with you."

"That's interesting. Usually Helena calls if it's important. Wonder what could be on his mind."

"Hi Werner," said Klaus." Helena had to run to town this morning. She asked me to phone you and Albert and inquire about your farm taxes. When are they due?"

"The first of next month."

"Do you have the money to pay them?"

"No, but I'm hoping the County will give me an extension just as the bank did."

"I know you don't like to accept charity, but Helena and I would like to pay your taxes, and also Albert's—*just this year.* We know it's been a bad year for weather and crops and we thought a little help would be a good thing. You're still on your own with the mortgage but we'd be glad if you would accept this gift. How about it?"

"Thanks a lot, Klaus. Of course it would be a big help and Laura and I appreciate your kind offer. But you would have to let us pay you back."

"If you have the money some day and want to repay, okay. But we'd be happy if you let us help you just this once."

Werner and Laura had to admit that her parents' offer was a godsend. They had reached a point where they didn't know what to do. Now at least they had a little breathing room, even if difficult days still lay ahead.

The forecasters were right again. Due to the heat, drought and dust storms of 1937 the crop yields averaged only about twenty percent of what they had been averaging in the past. If things didn't change they would be facing the same problems the following year, except double.

The question confronting all the farmers that fall was, "What will the weather be like next summer?"

6. Kids' World

On an April day the next spring Dale looked out the living room window and exclaimed, "Wow, look at that rain come down!"

Rain was falling on thirsty fields and the land quickly absorbed every drop.

"I sure hope the cycle of drought is over and done," said Werner.

It wasn't unusual for farm children to discuss such matters with their parents because they were part of the team. Adults and children worked together which helped the kids feel needed and gave them a sense of belonging.

Sometimes parents assigned adult responsibilities to the kids. When the boys were helping with field work, Werner and George occasionally asked them to drive the tractor or George's pickup. After driving in open fields it was an easy transition for the boys to begin driving on gravel roads. Not having a driver's license didn't seem to be an issue on the farm.

Here's an example. Late one Saturday afternoon Werner asked Ron, "Do you think you could drive Steve home for the weekend?"

"Sure, Dad. I'll be real careful."

The round trip totaled four miles with a few hills to negotiate along the way. Though only ten at the time, Ron was pleased with the amount of responsibility his father had given him. Of course

Laura would never have approved if she had known. Ron drove with utmost care and made the trip safely. He felt proud.

The parents needed the children's help in doing chores twice a day. Werner and Steve fed the horses, cattle and hogs. A windmill pumped water into a large tank for those animals. Meanwhile Laura and the kids fed and watered the chickens and geese as well as Rex and the cats. Eddie helped Sarah gather eggs because he liked to watch hens lay their eggs in a nest. "Watch this," he said to Sarah as he caught an egg in his hand at the precise moment it popped out of the hen. The family ate a few of the eggs but most they packed in cases and sold.

It wasn't unusual to hear Werner say, "C'mon everybody, let's milk the cows." This last chore they did in the barn. Everyone able to handle a stool and a pail joined in milking seven or eight cows by hand. Frequently a cat sat nearby hoping one of the kids would turn the cow's teat and squirt milk into its mouth.

"Here kitty, have a little supper," joked Ron.

The cat didn't seem to mind if it splashed all over its face.

Afterwards they poured the milk into a separator which the kids took turns operating manually with a handle. Electricity powered the separator when it became available. Cream came out of one spout and skimmed milk out the other. The cream they sold and much of the skimmed milk they gave to the hogs and chickens.

None of the farm buildings were more than a hundred feet from the house. The barn and crib sat to the north and west of the house and the chicken coops to the north and east. Each building had a unique smell, often unpleasant due to animal waste. But when Werner and the boys hauled the manure away and replaced it with fresh straw, the smell improved dramatically! The worst odor came from the nearby hog lot where the pigs dropped much of their excrement. Laura banished from the house anyone who approached with hog waste on his shoes.

One morning Werner announced, "Hey gang, it's a nice cool day. I'll bet you know what that means."

"Yup. I suppose it means pulling more cockleburs," replied Ron with very little enthusiasm.

This was another task for which the parents needed the kids' help. As they walked between the rows of corn or soybeans each person was responsible for a few rows, pulling or chopping out any unwanted intruders such as cockleburs and thistles. As long as the weather remained cool it was a pleasant job with lots of conversation flowing back and forth. But if it was a hot day it became an exhausting experience.

"I'll bet you a nickel I pull more weeds than you do on this round," Dale said to Ron hoping a little rivalry would take away the boredom.

"You're on," replied Ron. They soon discovered it was impossible to keep an accurate count when there were so many weeds.

Some farmers chose not to "walk" the fields because it seemed like too much work. Usually they regretted that decision when the weeds went to seed in the fall and came up with double infestation the next spring.

Farm researchers discovered pesticides which killed destructive plants and insects but did little or no damage to the crop. Later Werner and George read reports indicating that such pesticides could make the farmer ill or harm animals which consumed the grain. Consequently scientists developed effective but less toxic substances, only to discover that new strains of insects and weeds had invaded. And so the circle went round and around!

Werner felt relieved to see the weather improve during the summer of 1938. On a quiet evening he could hear the corn literally popping in the field as the stalks broke loose and shot upward. Yet the heat index remained higher and the rainfall lower than average. Although the crops would probably be better than the previous two years, it remained doubtful they would be sufficient to put the farmers back on track financially.

With that on his mind Werner was totally unprepared for an announcement Laura made one evening. "I know you may not agree with me, Honey," she said, "but I think we should *finally* get running water in our house."

"Are you serious? You're usually the conservative one in our family when it comes to finances, and you know how far behind we are in our payments to the bank. We simply don't have the money for such a big project right now."

"I know, but if we wait until we have the extra money we'll *never* get running water. And there are ways to cut down the cost."

"How so?"

"Claire Johnson told me they did some of the work themselves. Norm and Steve dug the trenches for the water pipes. George and Steve could help us."

"What if the bank gets impatient and says 'no more extensions'?"

"That's a long term problem we'll have to face. I know it won't be easy, Dear, but we'll struggle through it."

Werner wondered if Laura might be considering another loan from her parents and he didn't want that. Finally he said, "Let's think about it, Honey. We'll talk about it again tomorrow."

Werner didn't sleep well that night. He had serious worries about his debt to the bank and even the possibility of losing the 80 acres. On the other hand he felt concern about his wife and family. *"In a serious emergency my father would probably offer a temporary loan,"* he thought.

Before he went to sleep he decided he would go against his own instincts this time and go along with Laura's instead. *"I'll be saying a lot of prayers for favorable weather and a good harvest,"* he mused. The next morning he shared his feelings with Laura and of course she was very excited.

Once the decision was made things happened quickly. Werner employed a plumbing firm from Webster City to do the job. After drilling a new well near the house they dug a pit in which they placed the pump, a pressurized holding tank, and the electric motor. Fortunately electricity had been connected a year and a half earlier. Werner, George, Steve and the boys dug the trenches for the water pipes. Finally a bathroom was built inside the house and plumbing fixtures were installed.

After waiting so long the family seemed surprised that such a big project had been completed in such a short time. Everyone felt happy. At last they had running water!

"Just think," said Eddie, "now we can take a bath in a *real* bathtub instead of that round metal tub."

"What I like is our new bathroom," added Sarah. "It'll be so nice in the winter because we won't have to go outside to that cold outhouse."

Joining in the litany of gratitude Laura said, "I appreciate not having a pail of water and a ladle on the kitchen counter. With just a twist of the faucet I can get all the fresh water I want."

"We have the same convenience outside," stated Werner. "Instead of the old hand operated well we now have a pipe and a faucet. All you have to do is lift the handle on the faucet and presto, you get a pail of cold water."

All agreed they were happy and grateful for the wonderful gifts of running water and indoor plumbing. If only they could pay for it on the spot!

"I'm bored," complained Dale one uneventful afternoon. Isolation frequently presented a challenge for farm children. Friends their age lived a mile or more away and seeing them required a lengthy bicycle ride. What's amazing though is the ingenious manner in which they created activities and entertainment for themselves.

Most everything they did could be turned into a competition making it more fun. Who could finish his or her chores first? Who could get to the mailbox first after the postman stopped at the box a quarter mile away?

"I dare you to try this!" shouted Dale as he jumped on the back of a half grown calf and held on for dear life as it galloped across the pasture.

"Who would even want to do that? You're crazy," sneered Ron as he laughed.

The other kids were more cautious than Dale, probably a good thing because some competitions proved to be dangerous and led to injuries.

Dale and Ron liked to build things out of discarded lumber. They made Rex happy by building him a dog house. Situated under a large shade tree in the front yard and carpeted with old blankets, it was a cool retreat in the summer and a warm haven in the winter. But when it was extremely cold in the winter Rex was permitted to sleep in a back corner of the kitchen on those same old blankets.

Aware of the children's isolation Laura and Werner looked for excursions which the family could enjoy together. It excited the kids whenever their parents considered a trip to the county fair, a nearby circus, a movie in town, or an evening of fishing. On the way home from the county fair the kids usually engaged in debate about which attraction was the best.

"I liked the animals and their babies," said Sarah.

"I think the Octopus ride was the most fun," insisted Eddie. "It spun around so fast it made me dizzy."

Dale jumped in and added, "I loved the machinery. Did you see that new combine, Dad? I wonder if it'll put an end to the threshing machine some day."

"It very well could," replied Werner.

"Am I the only one who liked the medical science exhibit?" asked Ron.

Laura's weekly grocery shopping trips also provided outings for the children. Often they went along in order to break the routine. They liked going into stores to see the merchandise, especially the Five and Dime Store because it sold items they could afford. Sometimes they brought along their own money and bought a small toy or souvenir. A plastic ring which gave off a bright green glow in the dark caught Eddie's eye. It resembled one that Dale got from the cowboy star Tom Mix by mailing in a cereal box top. Eddie bought his ring for a dime which he considered a bargain.

"Anyone in the mood for an ice cream cone before we go home?" Laura inquired with a grin, knowing full well what the response would be.

"You bet!" exclaimed the kids. Laura offered this treat occasionally since it was not an expensive tradition. Cones cost just just a nickle. They called it "Cone for Home."

Another popular outing was fishing and the kids were happy when their parents agreed to take them. "I'm glad we have a couple neat rivers near our home," said Sarah.

The Boone River flowed through Webster City and the Des Moines River through Fort Dodge. A wooded bank on the side of either of those rivers provided a perfect spot from which to catch a few catfish or bullheads. When eaten directly from the frying pan they tasted great.

As usual Ron and Dale competed to see who could catch the most fish. Sarah and Eddie on the other hand worked together, helping each other bait the hook and land the fish. Their personalities complemented each other, Eddie being gregarious and cooperative and Sarah a free spirit who always spoke her mind openly.

Sometimes that put her at odds with her dad and made it more difficult for him to tell his little girl how much he loved her. Both were drawn to each other, yet sparks often flew. As for Ron and Laura, they were the peacemakers.

"Hey, how many fish did you catch?" asked Dale.

"Two," replied Ron.

"Sorry, I caught three," Dale boasted with a snicker.

"Stop bragging," Sarah interrupted. "Eddie and I caught four!"

Laura and Werner also snagged several but didn't say a word. They just smiled, packed up their gear and started back to the car. The next day the family had an excellent fish fry which tasted even better since they had caught the fish themselves.

The Schaub kids loved animals. After a cat gave birth to a litter of kittens Sarah summoned the family to watch them having a meal at the tummy of their mother. "Aren't they adorable?" she cooed. Everyone agreed.

But the boys believed baby pigs and calves were just as cute. Furthermore, as pigs matured they became very intelligent and curious.

"Look at this little guy," said Ron pointing at a young pig. "He's staring at me as if he wants to talk."

"And look at his ears pointing straight up," said Dale.

"He looks almost like Rex," added Eddie.

The kids hated to see any creature suffer. Although the farm animals were well cared for and generally had a good life, there were times when they experienced severe pain. For example young male pigs were castrated if they were headed for market, and they squealed loudly because the surgery took place without anesthesia. Similarly it was necessary to cut off the horns of some cows if they grew too long. The poor animal was tied down securely and the horns were cut off with a saw. Since cattle have nerves in their horns just as humans do in their teeth, it's not surprising that the unfortunate victim uttered loud moans of anguish. The operation looked even worse when blood flowed down the head of the cow from the severed horn—an ugly experience for both cattle and humans.

"Why do we have to do that?" asked Eddie angrily.

"I wish it weren't necessary," replied his dad. "I know it hurts them a lot but in the long run it helps."

"How?"

"If a cow's horns are allowed to grow too long, eventually they'll cause injuries to the other cattle or even to themselves. They can also get hung up in fences and other obstacles. Believe me, they'll be happier cows later on." Eddie accepted his dad's explanation but did not seem fully convinced.

On rare occasions a pregnant cow had serious pain and difficulty during the birth of its calf. When that happened Werner and Steve tried to help the mother by pulling on the hoofs of the calf. Usually that produced the desired result. However one birth was so difficult that no amount of pulling seemed to work.

"The cow is in a lot of distress and not doing well," observed Werner. "I think we better call a vet."

When the veterinarian arrived he tied a soft rope to the calf's hoofs and asked Steve and Werner to pull firmly but gently on it. At the same time he reached deep inside the cow and tried to maneuver the calf. After a short time it slipped out and immediately the proud but exhausted mother began licking and cleaning it. As soon as Werner helped the trembling newborn to its feet it began to suckle its mother. Ron and Dale watched the entire drama unfold and stood motionless, filled with awe and amazement.

"Wow! Did you see what I just saw?" said Dale.

"I sure did," answered Ron. "I didn't realize a birth could be so hard. That's scary!"

Frigid weather brought another kind of suffering to the animals. During the winter it was common to see a group of cattle standing close to one another in a circle, shivering in the cold. The barn and chicken coops helped protect against the elements, but the buildings were still cold inside when the temperature became exceptionally frigid outside.

One night it was nearly ten degrees below zero. Werner said to Steve, "Let's hang a few heat lights in the barn stalls where the sows are nursing their babies. Otherwise I'm afraid we'll have some dead piglets in the morning."

Yet, in spite of cold weather many hardy animals enjoyed running outside and frolicking in the snow when the temperatures moderated.

A number of animals had to be slaughtered for food each year. "Do we really *have* to do this?" pleaded Sarah as the family gathered a group of chickens for butchering.

"I'm afraid so, Sweetheart," answered her mother. "We do have to eat." Although reluctant, the children understood such drastic action was necessary.

Working together they captured, decapitated, de-feathered and cleaned a group of young roosters. Hens were spared so they could continue to produce eggs. The same procedure was followed with geese except their down feathers were saved for use in pillows and bedding.

When Werner slaughtered a mature calf he hired a professional butcher to do the slicing and packaging. He and Laura then took the packaged meat to town and placed it in a rented box in a large commercial freezer, making it possible for them to pick up packages of frozen meat whenever they were in town. Junking the old ice box, they bought a small electric refrigerator and kept a few packages of meat in the freezing compartment at all times.

"It's wonderful to be able to get fresh meat whenever I want," said Laura.

"And if our refrigerator gets empty we can always find another young rooster outside," added Werner.

"That's one good thing about living on a farm. Fresh food is always available."

Wild animals were different. Farmers considered some a bane and others a blessing. For example they relied on birds and bees to help with the pollination process, but they hated corn borers and rodents which destroyed crops.

"I like skunks. They're cute," commented Eddie. Nevertheless everyone avoided them for obvious reasons. More than once Rex and the boys got too close to a skunk and were hit with its terrible smelling spray. As they approached the house Laura said, "Stop! Don't come inside until you first take off your clothes and take a bath. And be sure to keep Rex outside!" Weasels liked to eat both chickens and eggs so their presence around the coops stirred fear among the flock. The responsibility of sniffing them out and keeping them at bay was assigned to Rex. In spite of the way he smelled after his encounter with the skunk, he remained a valuable and treasured partner.

The Schaub boys declared war on ground squirrels, small rodents about twice the size of chipmunks with similar coloring and black stripes running down their backs. They lived in holes which they burrowed into the ground. Though cute, they had the bad habit of digging up and eating seeds which had been planted in the fields. Therefore the boys considered them enemies and felt justified in hunting and killing them. Their method of extermination was direct and efficient.

"Hey, there's one over there!" shouted Eddie as he pointed to a ground squirrel standing high on its two back legs and surveying the horizon for danger. Dale and Rex gave chase but it quickly darted into its nearby hole.

"Got the water?" asked Dale.

"Yup, here it is," said Ron as he began pouring a pail of water into the hole.

Quickly the ground squirrel poked up its head and gasped for air. Rex grabbed the little fellow in his jaws and dispatched it in a hurry. If Rex wasn't handy the boys used a club to terminate the poor creatures. Sometimes they felt guilty about such cruelty, but they dismissed that concern quickly reasoning that they had destroyed a pest which did damage to the crops.

One afternoon Helena and Klaus stopped for a visit. As they were leaving Grandma Bauer said to the boys, "I hear you guys are pretty good at hunting ground squirrels. I'd like to hire you to get rid of some of ours. I'll pay you a nickel for each one you destroy. Are you interested?"

Ron and Dale readily agreed. Eddie grabbed Laura's hand and pleaded, "Can I go too, Mom?"

"Of course, dear."

"Goodie!" he exclaimed.

The next day Laura drove the boys and Rex to Grandma's and Grandpa's house. From there they proceeded directly to the pasture and began hunting for their unsuspecting prey. Netting only seven that afternoon, they didn't consider their mission very successful. Not known for her generosity Grandma Bauer gave each of them a dime and thanked them heartily for their efforts.

Eddie already knew his multiplication tables. "But Grandma," he protested, "you promised to give us a nickel for each ground squirrel and we got seven. Seven times five is thirty-five and you gave us only thirty cents. Don't you still owe us a nickel?"

"You're right, Eddie, here's another nickel. I just thought it would be hard to divide a nickel three ways."

Later Klaus took Ron aside and secretly handed him a dollar bill. "Take this," he said. "When you get home divide it between the three of you boys and tell the others not to say anything, okay?"

"Okay Grandpa. Thanks a lot!"

Two words described Grandpa Klaus: kind and generous.

Though the kids despised a few wild animals they dearly loved others. One of them was a pigeon whose mother had been killed. Ron noticed a few nests in the hayloft so he climbed up to investigate. There he discovered one with a baby pigeon huddled inside, trembling and frightened. With care he lifted the tiny bird out of the nest and carried it to the house.

"Oh, how sweet he is!" exclaimed Sarah, unconsciously assigning the male gender to the bird. "I want to adopt him."

"Me too. Can we keep him, Mom?" begged Eddie.

After pondering a few seconds Laura answered, "I suppose it would be all right if you promise two things: you won't allow him inside the house, and the two of you will be completely responsible for his care. Can you agree to that?"

"Sure Mom. We promise. We'll take care of everything. Thanks a lot!" said Sarah gratefully.

She and Eddie made a soft bed for the little pigeon inside a box, which they placed in the front porch where no other animals had access except Rex. The cats were not allowed in the porch.

Eddie said, "I wonder what we should call him."

"Since he's a pigeon how about naming him "Pidgie?"

"That's okay with me."

They put water and seeds in the box but Pidgie didn't eat. It became apparent they would have to force feed him. Taking turns, Sarah and Eddie held his beak open with one hand while putting small seeds into his mouth with the other. After a couple weeks he started eating on his own and then grew quickly. Before long he began flapping his wings. One day he finally took off on his maiden flight which lasted only several seconds.

"What should we do now?" Eddie wondered. "What if he flies away?"

"I'm worried about that too," replied Sarah. "I don't want to put him in a cage because that would be like a prison. I want him to have his freedom. Guess we'll just have to hope for the best."

"Please don't leave us, Pidgie," Eddie pleaded sadly.

The children needn't have worried because bonding had taken place. Not only did Pidgie stay but he made himself right at home. When a few people were having a conversation outside, it wasn't long before the young pigeon landed on someone's shoulder and welcomed himself into the group. A salesman arrived one day and was knocking at the door when Pidgie tried to land on his head. That so startled the salesman that he ran to his car and left in a hurry!

Since the enclosed front porch had been the pigeon's initial home, he chose it for his bedroom. Earlier Werner had driven a few long nails partially into the inside wall of the porch to serve as jacket hangers and Pidgie chose one of those as his perch, roosting on it every night.

The pigeon lived with the Schaubs for approximately a year. One Sunday noon when they returned home from church Eddie looked for Pidgie but couldn't find him. Everyone became concerned and joined in the search. Suddenly Dale shouted, "Hey guys, come over here. I think I've discovered something."

Scattered in a small circle lay a bunch of feathers which looked disturbingly familiar. It appeared one of the cats found the pigeon just too tempting. Poor Pidgie trusted everyone and everything without reservation. In the end it cost him his life.

Every member of the family was sad but no one more than Sarah and Eddie. They ran away crying, looking for a place to grieve in private.

In spite of that mini-tragedy Werner couldn't help feeling thankful and optimistic when he looked at his fields. After two years of extreme heat and drought the summer of 1938 provided considerably more rain and sunshine. "*The crops may not be perfect but they sure look good*," he thought.

He hoped that a bountiful harvest would enable him not only to pay for the previous year's loan extension but also to make a partial payment for the present year. Recently the bank sent him a letter urging immediate payment of the loan extension. Also he still owed money for the machinery he purchased. His financial worries were far from over.

The time for another alfalfa harvest arrived. As Steve was cutting the hay he suddenly stopped, jumped off the tractor and ran back to the mower. After examining the sickle bar he waved to Ron and Dale to come and help. They approached on the run and asked what happened.

"The mower hit this pheasant hen and killed her. She was sitting on her nest in the midst of the alfalfa. Maybe she was trying to protect her eggs. Do you think your parents would like to have the pheasant for a meal?"

"I don't think so," replied Ron, "but I'd like to take the eggs and put them under one of our chicken hens."

"That's just what I was thinking," said Dale.

The hen accepted the eggs as if they were her own and sat on them faithfully. Before long they hatched and six baby pheasants followed their proud adoptive mother around the yard, picking up any seeds they could find. Since pheasants are fast runners the hen soon found it difficult to keep up with her children.

On a cloudy afternoon Ron and Dale spotted the white hen running as fast as she could on a black plowed field some distance from the house. She was trying without much success to keep up with the young birds who were darting back and forth looking for food. Suddenly that night the hen died, probably from exhaustion, leaving the six small pheasants behind as orphans.

"I've got an idea," said Dale. "Let's build a small house for the pheasants?"

"Good thought," Ron replied. "We can put it under the shade tree in the back yard and build a wire mesh fence around it."

"We should make the fence long so the pheasants have room to run."

"Okay, but we'll have to cover the top with fencing too. Otherwise they'll fly out."

Building on the ideas of each other, the boys finished their plan and in just a few days completed the project. With a final stroke of genius they painted the little house white so it would match the color of their white frame home.

Dale said to Ron, "Why don't we use Pidgie's pans?"

"That'll work. You put water in one and I'll get grain for the other."

Finally they brought the six orphans from their temporary cage and turned them loose inside the fence. It didn't take long for them to adjust to their new environment and begin eating. A couple weeks later they even ate seeds from the kids' hands when offered. Still, they retained a wild instinct and were uncomfortable whenever a human tried to touch them.

Gradually they reached maturity and began flapping their wings and running back and forth inside the fence.

"Looks like they want to fly," Ron observed.

"I'm afraid so," said Dale. "I hate to say it but I think we should let them go."

Although Sarah and Eddie pleaded with them not to do it, the boys released them the following morning. When they opened the fence the pheasants walked out and looked around cautiously. They appeared to be confused by their freedom. At last one of them ran a short distance and began to fly. Immediately the others rose in flight and followed their leader. Soon they were out of sight. With a tear in her eye Sarah remarked, "I wonder if we'll ever see them again."

As it turned out the Schaubs did see the pheasants again—many times. For the rest of that summer they returned every evening at about six o'clock and landed on the hog lot where the pigs had been eating corn. For nearly ten minutes they ate their fill of kernels which the hogs left behind. Then they flew off as quietly and quickly as they had come.

One evening the pheasants flew away toward the west just as the sun was setting in a blaze of orange. Laura said, "Isn't that a beautiful sight? I feel as if we're in the middle of creation watching it happen."

Inspired by his mother Ron stated, "This is better than watching a movie in town. We do have some neat experiences on the farm."

7. Faith and Community

"Careful Dear, some cattle are on the road up ahead," cautioned Laura.

"I see that," said Werner. "Looks like some of them are having a good meal in the oats field across the road."

The Schaubs were driving to church on a Sunday morning when they noticed the straying cows. Possibly their neighbor left a gate unlatched when he and his family went to church earlier. Werner stopped the car and said, "C'mon everybody. Let's see if we can chase these critters back into their pen."

He and the boys rounded up the cattle in the oats field and urged them back across the road. Laura and Sarah stood on either side of the roadway to prevent them from making a detour. Soon all the cattle were back where they belonged and Werner latched the gate securely. However the roundup took almost a half hour and now it was too late to go to church. "May as well go back home," said Werner.

It felt strange not going to church. People in the farm community hardly ever missed a service whether they were Catholics or Protestants, not just because they were religious but also because the church was the center of their social lives. They frequently saw their neighbors at church functions such as ice cream socials, church league ball games, sewing circles, or even a New Year's Eve oyster stew vigil. Lifelong friendships evolved at such church community events.

After supper that evening Werner asked, "Any of you guys interested in going for a ride?"

"Sure, let's go!" they all responded positively.

Yet Laura and the kids were surprised because they rarely went for a ride without a good reason. It turned out Werner did have a purpose in mind. He drove directly to the parsonage next door to their rural church. There he and Laura chatted briefly with Pastor and Mrs. Larson while the kids used the swings on the playground. After telling the pastor about their cattle drama in the morning, Werner suggested that was the reason he and his family were absent from the worship service.

"You don't have to explain or apologize," replied Pastor Larson. "I'm sure you realize that helping your neighbor is an act of worship in itself."

Eddie overheard the pastor's words and they made an indelible impression on him. He never forgot them and frequently quoted them. For the rest of his life he considered loving one's neighbor equally as important as attending a church service.

The Schaubs reentered their car and prepared to return home. Before leaving Werner asked, "Are we doing the Corn Mission Program again this year, Pastor?"

"We certainly are. We already have six loads."

"Make it seven. I'll take mine to the grain elevator in the morning."

Because the congregation struggled every year to meet its budget, the members adopted a Corn Mission Program to make sure they'd always meet their pledge to world missions and local benevolences. It was a unique but simple idea. Each farmer agreed to take a wagon load of shelled corn to the grain elevator, approximately one hundred bushels, and credit it to the church mission account. Those few who were not farmers donated cash instead. After adopting this plan the church never again failed to meet its mission commitments, even when it struggled with its local expenses—including the pastor's salary!

As in all institutions contradictions were apparent in this small rural church. On the one hand its members were good people, kind, forgiving and compassionate, as might be expected considering their beliefs. Yet they lived by religious rules which sometimes proved to be stern and rigid. The experience of a young member named Priscilla serves as an example.

While still single and living at home, Priscilla became pregnant and in the course of time gave birth to a baby boy. After the baby arrived the young father removed himself from the picture.

Priscilla and her parents decided they would work together in loving and raising her little son. Yet in the eyes of the church she had sinned. Since the alleged wrongdoing had become public knowledge it was a public offense. Therefore the church elders asked her to stand before the assembled congregation and repent so that her offense could be publicly forgiven. Though extremely difficult to do, she bravely faced the congregation and tearfully apologized. After that no one ever brought up the incident again, at least in public.

Some good did come out of the experience however. Priscilla fulfilled her promise to nurture her son "in the Lord." From that time forward the people of the congregation not only forgave Priscilla but also surrounded her and her son with their love and support. He grew up beautifully and was fully accepted into the fellowship of the boys and young men at the church.

———

It was a warm summer afternoon when the phone rang. Laura answered with an uneasy feeling. People didn't often call at that time of day, and her intuition proved to be correct.

"Hello Laura. This is Betty McDonald. I'm afraid I have some very bad news. I wanted to tell you right away."

Laura felt a lump in the pit of her stomach. "What happened?"

"Do you remember Debbie, George's niece?"

"Of course I do."

"There's been an accident." Betty's voice wavered. "A large truck hit her car broadside."

"Oh no! Is she—is she all right?"

"No Laura. She's gone. Our wonderful niece died instantly."

"I'm so sorry. How shocking! Is there anything we can do to help? Anything at all?"

"No, I—well, maybe. The service will be at our church. Even though you aren't Catholic I think it would mean a lot to George's family if you and other folks from your congregation would come."

"We'll be there. Be assured of that."

Betty was quiet for a moment. "Do you think Ron would be able to spend a little extra time with Tom? He could use a friend right now. He and Debbie were very close."

"Of course. He'd want to do that anyway." Laura wiped away a tear. "Werner and I are here if you need anything—anything at all."

The next day the newspaper reported the accident including pictures of the horrible crash. Laura had heard that Debbie, only seventeen, always tried to be a very careful driver. That made the tragedy all the more difficult to understand. Apparently she was making a left turn off the highway and mistakenly assumed the on-coming truck was going to do the same. Though she was not being careless it was a fatal mistake.

Sadly many teenage farm boys did *not* always try to be careful drivers. They loved the thrill of traveling at high speeds on gravel roads, even when hills made it impossible to see on-coming traffic. Sensational reports of highway tragedies appeared all too frequently in the newspaper.

"Thanks so much for coming," Betty said to Laura after the funeral service. "George and I appreciate your and Werner's support. By the way Tom was thrilled when Ron came over last evening."

"I know you and George would be there for us under similar circumstances. How are George's brother and his family doing?"

"It's difficult. Life will never be the same for them."

A large number of people from neighboring non-Catholic congregations attended the service, demonstrating the good will existing between the various churches in the area. An ecumenical spirit flourished among them, not so much in liturgy and theology as in friendship and respect.

—∞∞—

The younger generation also experienced this community spirit, especially at school. By this time all the Schaub children had transferred to the Lutheran parochial school for religious and confirmation instruction. During recess many of the boys and girls developed lifelong relationships as they joined together in sport activities such as softball, kickball, sledding and ice skating. Though they would never admit it the older boys and girls began to notice each other in a special way, the way young people do at that age! Of course sex education didn't exist then and the subject was rarely discussed either at home or in school. Sadly young people were on their own for that part of their education.

The teacher Mr. Hemming, one of two, was a kind man, respected by everyone but also strict. Greg, one of the student clowns, learned the hard way just how strict. One morning he brought a dead rat to school, tied a nearly invisible fish line to its tail and hid it in a front corner of the room. As Mr. Hemming taught a class Greg, sitting at his desk, slowly pulled the fish line. The dead rat slid silently across the floor near the spot where the teacher was standing. As fate would have it Mr. Hemming noticed Greg's hands pulling in the fish line. The punishment was swift and just.

"Greg, would you like to suggest a fair penalty for your actions?" asked Mr. Hemming.

"No sir."

"Then I'm going to ask you to write a 300 word essay on everything there is to know about rats. Is that agreeable?"

"Yes sir."

"Do you think you can give me that essay by tomorrow morning?"

"I'll try, sir."

"Good. And will that be the end of rat presentations?"

"Absolutely, sir."

Needless to say Greg wished he had never conceived the idea of a dead rat trick.

———❧———

Everyone in the church loved the Christmas program presented jointly by children of the weekday school and Sunday School. After weeks of rehearsing the children presented their songs and recitations at the Christmas Eve worship service. During the service the ushers distributed to each child a brown paper bag containing unshelled peanuts and two oranges, a truly modest gift. Yet that simple gift delighted the children beyond belief.

On Christmas Eve in 1938 Eddie faced a perplexing question: is there a Santa Claus? At the age of seven he still believed in Santa though many of his classmates at school did not. Eddie decided he would try to settle the question once and for all.

A few days before Christmas as the family gathered for supper Eddie asked, "Would you guys help me with an experiment?"

"Sure, Honey. What would you like us to do?" replied his mom.

"On Christmas Eve I'd like everybody to get into the car at the same time—except me. I want to make one last trip into the house to make sure no one has put any presents under the tree. Then I'll come to the car and we can all go to church."

"Who would put anything under the tree?" Ron asked.

"I don't know," said Eddie. "But when we come back from church I want to be the first one to go into the house and look under the tree. If there are no toys, then there's no Santa. But if there *are* presents, then we'll know for sure there's a Santa Claus."

"Sounds like a good idea," said his dad. "Let's try it." They all agreed.

On Christmas Eve everything seemed to go as Eddie planned. When the family arrived back home after the service he ran into the house at full speed. When he looked under the tree he was amazed and happy to see a bunch of shiny new toys. Because his experiment seemed to offer definite proof, Eddie continued to believe in Santa for almost another year. But eventually his doubts returned. Ron mercifully decided to explain the mystery.

"Eddie," he said, "do you remember your little experiment last Christmas Eve?"

"I sure do. I thought it worked great."

"Yes, some of it did, but some didn't."

"What do you mean?"

"I'm afraid Dad played a little trick on you. When you went into the house for your final inspection Dad sneaked through the kitchen and went upstairs. As you were coming out of the house Dad raced downstairs, dropped a few toys under the tree and came walking slowly from the garage as though nothing had happened. Then you both got into the car and you had no idea what he had done."

When Eddie learned the truth he was astonished and upset at first, but soon decided it was okay. He continued to believe in the spirit of Santa Claus for the rest of his life, the spirit of giving, sharing and loving. *"As long as those things are alive among us,"* he reasoned, *the spirit of Santa Claus is alive too!"*

As spring approached Werner felt strongly he needed a pickup truck on the farm. He learned from George that a farmer living near Webster City had purchased a new pickup and wanted to sell his old one at a reasonable price. Taking Steve with him, Werner drove to the man's home and asked about the truck. After a little negotiating he succeeded in buying it for only two hundred dollars. Though it was old and not in the best condition, it ran well and would serve Werner's needs for a while.

Werner and Steve returned home to share the news with Laura. However the reaction they received was different than what they expected.

"I can't believe you would buy a pickup without even mentioning it to me first," Laura complained.

Trying to defend himself Werner replied, "But we need a truck and it cost only two hundred dollars. I didn't want to lose the opportunity."

"We're in debt up to our necks already. I'd think you would at least talk to me about it first. Isn't that what a partnership is all about?"

"Of course it is, Honey. I'm sorry. I should have mentioned it to you before we left to go see the pickup."

"I'm trying to believe you, but this isn't the first time something like this has happened."

"You're absolutely right and I'm wrong. All I can do now is assure you that in the long run the pickup will save us more money than it cost today."

Werner's prediction probably came true. Although the years 1939 to 1941 were not exceptional, they proved to be at least average as far as weather, crops and income were concerned. During those years Werner and Laura managed to pay the balance of what they owed for machinery purchases and the installing of running water. They also reduced somewhat the amount they were in arrears to the bank for the mortgage. Though continuing to be patient because of Werner's regular payments, the bank nevertheless sent the Schaubs strong encouragements to get their account up to date. Regrettably these frequent notices robbed Werner and Laura of some of the joy they had experienced by making steady progress.

"We've felt the strain of financial pressure for a long time," observed Werner. "Looks like we'll have to live with it a little longer."

<hr />

Walking between the corn rows and pulling the despised cockleburs continued to be a regular activity. Dale thought it was strange the cockleburs didn't seem to suffer as much from the lack of rain as the crops did.

After supper one evening Steve said to Dale, "I think I'll make another round trip through the corn field while it's cool. Wanna come along?"

"Okay, but just one round." said Dale. He didn't really want to go but hated to say no to Steve.

As they reached the far end of the field Steve said, "Why don't we take off a few of our clothes and sit down for a while?" He began to take off his shirt and pants.

"Why should we do that?" objected Dale.

"Just to rest and cool off a bit."

"I'm not tired or hot. C'mon, let's head back home. It's getting dark."

"Be a sport. Just a little while."

"No! I'm heading back!"

"Oh all right," said Steve as he put his shirt back on and buckled his belt.

Although Dale didn't understand why, he felt extremely uncomfortable all the way home. With fear and anger clashing in his mind, he pulled weeds strenuously and didn't say a word. He was afraid to say anything to his parents and didn't want to get Steve in trouble. *"What if some of his fears were just his imagination?"* he wondered. In the end he resolved that he'd never say a word about the incident to anyone. And he never did.

———

Laura wanted to do something special for Ron and Dale's approaching birthdays. One balmy summer night as the moon bounced its soft light throughout the room, she lay in bed thinking about an exciting idea. *"Maybe tonight would be a good time to speak to Werner about it,"* she thought. She snuggled up to him and propped her elbow on the pillow.

"Honey, are you awake?"

"I am now," he chuckled.

"I've got a unique idea for the boys' birthdays."

"I'm almost afraid to ask," he muttered. "What is it?"

"They've been talking lately about wishing they had a pony. I'm wondering if we could give one to them and they could share it."

Werner turned towards her. "Well, that *is* interesting. As it happens, when I was in town yesterday I bumped into Norm Johnson. He asked how Steve was doing, and of course I said fine. Later in the conversation he mentioned wanting to sell one of his two ponies. Steve isn't home much anymore and Norm doesn't think they need to keep both of his boys' ponies. I told him I might be interested." He chuckled. "Imagine that. This time our minds have been running on the same track."

"How exciting!" exclaimed Laura as she patted his arm. "That's perfect! How much does Norm want?"

"Not that much. He said he'd sell the younger one for fifty dollars. That's a great price."

"Then it's settled," said Laura leaning down and kissing Werner on the cheek. "Let's do it for the boys."

"I'm amazed!" he joked. "What's happened to my conservative wife?"

When the day for the birthday celebrations arrived Werner said to Ron and Dale, "C'mon guys, I want to show you something in the barn."

Laura, Sarah and Eddie, knowing what was about to happen, followed behind. Werner opened the door to a pen and there stood a beautiful brown pony with a gray mane and tail, its ears erect.

"Happy Birthday!" they all shouted.

"Holy smoke!" Ron exclaimed. "I can't believe it!" said Dale. They said "thank you" again and again. After leading the pony outside each went for a short ride.

"He's frisky and fast," said Ron. "Any thoughts on what to name him?" he asked Dale.

"How about Frisky?"

"Okay by me."

The boys rode Frisky bareback with just a bridle. All he wanted to do was run fast. One day in an open field Dale pushed Frisky to run as fast as he could go. Driving alongside in the pickup, Werner clocked his speed at more than twenty five miles per hour. "Not bad for a little fellow," he noted.

Ron, Dale, and Tom had a lot of fun riding the pony. Poor Eddie felt sad he couldn't ride at all for a while. Frisky was too spirited and powerful for him to handle.

"Don't worry, Eddie," said Sarah sympathetically. "Now you and I get the bike all to ourselves!"

The spirit of faith and community strengthened and unified the farmers of northwest Iowa. The Schaub's smaller family community consisted of the parents and four children, Steve Johnson, Frisky, Rex, several cats, and the rest of the animals. All lived and played together, supported one another, and liked each other—most of the time! All considered faith, love and community to be important ingredients in their lives.

8. War and Prosperity

It was a sunny bright Sunday in December. After arriving home from church Laura prepared a delicious fried chicken dinner with apple pie for dessert.

"That sure was a fantastic meal, Honey," said Werner, patting his stomach. All the children thought so too.

Radio music was playing in the background when suddenly a special report interrupted the program and caught everybody's attention. Speaking in ominous tones the announcer exclaimed, "At eight o'clock this morning, Hawaii time, a large number of Japanese war planes bombed the United States naval fleet and Air base at Pearl Harbor on the island of Oahu, Hawaii. Damage is extensive. Several battleships are on fire and hundreds of lives have been lost. Stay tuned for further reports." In a matter of seconds a beautiful Sunday was transformed into a "day of infamy."

"How terrible!" said Laura . The disturbing news deeply shook her and Werner and left Sarah and the boys speechless. Just ten at the time, Eddie felt a little different. Though he knew the news was bad, he also found it interesting. It excited his imagination as he thought about all those planes and ships in action. Outside he felt the sun's warmth and everything seemed peaceful and calm to him. Standing there in the beauty of God's creation, it was hard for him to comprehend the tragedy that was taking place thousands of miles away in beautiful Hawaii.

The phone rang. Laura lifted the receiver and said hello.

"Hi Laura. This is Betty McDonald again with more bad news. Have you heard the radio reports?"

"Yes, isn't it awful? Werner says the war will probably spread to more countries. It makes me ill just to think about it."

"I feel the same way. George and I believe it might be good if a group of us neighbors got together and talked about it. Would you folks be interested in coming to our home tonight?"

"That sounds like a good idea. What time shall we come?"

"Let's make it seven thirty. I'm so glad you can come. By the way, Tom asked me to mention that you should bring your kids along, especially Ron of course. I'm going to invite the Johnson family too."

The meeting was helpful. Both adults and children were able to vent some of their anxieties and offer encouragement to one another. Betty mentioned there would be a prayer service the following evening at their church with invitations extended to everyone, not just Catholics. George, who had undergone horrific experiences as a soldier during World War I, said, "We're all going to pray for an early end to the war. Also for the protection of our kids in the military." Everyone felt somewhat better as they headed back home.

Norm and Claire Johnson worried that Steve would be among the first to be drafted. However during his medical exam the doctors discovered a torn cartilage in his right knee and declared him "4-F." Meanwhile the McDonalds and Schaubs were relieved that their oldest sons were just fifteen and sophomores in high school. Surely the war would be over before they turned eighteen and became subject to the draft, or at least that was their hope.

Barry Miller, a young man who lived with his parents on a nearby farm, had an entirely different outlook. He was nineteen and *wanted* to join the Marines. He feared they wouldn't accept him because of a limp he had acquired in an incident five years earlier. At the time it happened he was a fun-loving mischievous teenager with a big smile that stretched from ear to ear.

One summer evening, "just for a little excitement," Barry contrived a plan to sneak into a neighbor's garden and steal a watermelon. It was dusk when he crawled into the garden on his hands and knees. Unfortunately the owner, an ill-tempered man, spotted him wrestling with a large melon. Resolving to "teach that kid a lesson," he went into the house and got his small shotgun. It was his intention just to scare the young intruder, so he aimed about twenty feet to one side of Barry and pulled the trigger. The quiet evening was shattered with a blast so loud it scared the poor teenage thief half to death. Although the shot missed him, a couple tiny pellets strayed and hit his right knee. Leaving the watermelon behind, he held back his tears as he hobbled home. For the rest of his life he walked with a slight limp.

Now five years later Barry wanted to enlist and help defend his country. He couldn't stop worrying that the Marine Corps would reject him. During his medical exam he hid his limp as much as possible, and to his surprise the Marines accepted him. After fighting valiantly on several South Pacific islands, he returned home after the war with several medals pinned on his chest. Frequently thereafter his friends teased him by calling him "the limping Marine." Barry didn't mind. He took it as a compliment and just flashed that big smile of his from ear to ear.

Werner didn't like government rationing but he realized it was necessary. Materials needed for the war effort, such as sugar and gasoline for example, had to be strictly limited.

Werner and countless others often left their cars in the garage because their gas tanks were empty. However many enterprising farmers found ways to get around the rules. Since agricultural production was a high priority, tanker trucks routinely delivered plenty of gasoline to farmers for their tractors—no questions asked. But many used some of that "agriculture" gas in their cars, a temptation too difficult to resist. As Werner pumped some into his Chevy he muttered to himself, *I hope the government and the good Lord understand.*

Farm kids helped the war effort by collecting all kinds of scrap metal, from tooth paste containers and tin cans to broken pieces of machinery. "I'm amazed this junk can be turned into a tank or a plane," said Eddie.

Although the war didn't greatly change the lives of the children, it was in their thoughts constantly. After a major battle such as the D-Day invasion they read about it in the newspaper devouring every detail. Sarah said, "They make me sad sometimes, but I like the news reports in the movie theaters."

Dale and Eddie had fun making model war planes, especially the ones which came in cereal boxes and required a penny in the nose cone. "Look how well it flies!" exclaimed Dale as he tossed one across the living room. Before long the boys could identify almost every American and enemy plane in use during the war.

In most things the kids followed their normal routines. Though only an eighth grader, Dale often drove Sarah, Eddie and himself to their church school in the pickup. Ron and Tom rode a bus to their high school in town.

Early in 1942 Norm Johnson phoned Werner and said, "I've been wondering if you could manage without Steve after your boys get out of school in the spring. Recently I've needed more help myself. Of course Steve could continue working for you until school ends."

"The same thought crossed my mind," replied Werner. "Ron and Dale are now about the same age as Steve when he came to work for us. On a tractor they can accomplish nearly as much as any adult. So let's do what you said."

"Thanks Werner. Claire and I want you and Laura to know how much we appreciate what you've done for Steve. He's been a different person since he started working for you. Recently he even told me he'd like to see if he can still get the equivalent of a high school diploma."

"Steve did a great job for us," said Werner. "I think he'll make you proud some day."

Ron and Dale were happy when they heard about the new arrangement. They relished the idea of no longer being just "boys" but rather part of the adult team.

⚬⚬⚬⚬

One night before they went to sleep Werner said to Laura, "You know, Honey, this war is tragic for millions of people, but ironically it's helping us."

"In what way?"

"Our country and our allies desperately need everything we farmers produce. As a result we're getting higher prices for everything we sell. I'm actually beginning to see a tiny light at the end of the tunnel."

"That's great, dear. I'll bet it's a good feeling."

"It sure is. For the first time I feel a little financial security—even if we can't buy a lot of things we need because of the war."

"It makes me feel guilty though to think we're prospering while millions of other people are suffering and dying."

"I know. Some things are hard to understand. We need to be grateful for so many blessings."

"And keep praying for those devastated by the war," added Laura.

"If you don't mind I'd like to bring up something on a much happier note," said Werner.

"That might be a good thing. Go ahead," replied Laura.

"Would you like to go to the Saturday night dance at the town hall? It might be good for us to forget about the world situation for a few hours."

"That sounds like a nice idea. Kids are welcome at the dances too but I doubt Eddie would want to go. He could stay overnight with my parents."

The evening turned out to be just what the doctor ordered for the entire community. Everyone had a good time dancing, visiting with neighbors they hadn't seen for a while, and just letting their hair down. Seeking a break from the disheartening events taking place around the world proved to be a wise choice.

An amateur band provided music. At eleven o'clock a committee of women served desserts along with coffee and soda pop. The timing of refreshments was important because Roman Catholics could not eat or drink anything after midnight. Their rules of piety required that nothing should pass their lips on the "Lord's Day" until *after* they had received the bread of Holy Communion the next morning at church. Protestants didn't have such scruples and continued to enjoy food and drink until well after midnight!

Farm families also enjoyed parties in their homes during the war. Children liked them because they could run wild outside, and so did the men because an extra beverage could be added to the menu—beer!

Teen-agers didn't allow the war to interfere with their social life. They had little trouble finding something to do whether it was roller skating in town, going on a church sponsored hay ride, tobogganing or ice skating in the winter, or swimming in the summer.

Tobogganing became less popular for a while after a bad accident. Three girls were sliding down a hill at high speed when suddenly they crashed into a large rock hidden under the snow. Two of the girls were thrown clear but the third suffered severe injuries of the leg and knee, including two broken bones. The injuries required hospitalization and lengthy rehab.

Softball was one of the boys' favorite summer pastimes. After supper they frequently met in a pasture and played until dusk. Tom, Ron and a few other boys reached the age when they could get a driver's license and that presented all kinds of new possibilities for entertainment. They had fun "cruising" down the main street of Fort Dodge or Webster City, waving at friends or at girls they didn't know. Of course the car radio was blaring all the time.

Radio played a large role in entertaining teenagers. The older kids loved listening to music while Eddie and his friends preferred action programs like "The Lone Ranger" or mystery thrillers like "The Shadow." Werner and his sons considered it a great treat to gather around the radio and share the excitement of sporting events.

In the spring of 1944 Ron and Tom experienced two life changing events. First, they graduated from high school near the top of their class, filling their parents with pride.

"What are you planning to do next year?" George asked Ron.

"I'm hoping to go to the University of Iowa and study biology and medicine. I'd like to be a doctor."

"That sounds great. Best of luck to you."

"How about you, Tom?" asked Laura. "Any plans yet?"

"I'll probably go to Iowa State and major in mechanical engineering. I figure that'll help me get a good job when I graduate—unless I decide to join Dad on the farm."

"Fantastic! I'm sure you'll excel no matter what you do," said Werner.

The second event was scary. In midsummer not long after they turned eighteen, Tom and Ron received a letter from the draft board asking them to appear for a medical exam and possible induction into the Army. Concern flooded the hearts of their parents who had prayed that the war would be over by this time. It didn't help when they heard frightening reports of casualties during the D-Day invasion in France just six weeks earlier. Well over three thousand U.S. troops lost their lives the first day, a fearful statistic. The young men however accepted the news calmly. "Guess we may have to postpone our education plans for a while," said Ron.

As expected they passed their medical exams and "Uncle Sam" asked them to report for induction in one month.

The next day Ron phoned Tom and asked, "Got any ideas on sharing the news with the guys?"

"How about inviting them to a swim at Twin Lakes? We can tell them there."

"Excellent idea! Let's do it."

The swim party proved to be a perfect plan. In addition to being fun it gave the boys a good opportunity to break the news to their friends who had many questions: "When will you leave?" "Where will you go, east or west?" "How long do you think you'll be gone?" Unfortunately there weren't many answers.

A few days later Werner said to his family, "Since Ron will be leaving soon why don't we all do something together that's really fun?"

"Like what?" they asked.

"Well, I was thinking about spending a day at the State Fair in Des Moines. How would you feel about that?"

"I'd love it!" exclaimed Eddie. Everybody agreed it was a super idea.

Leaving early on a beautiful sunny morning, they made the trip to Des Moines in less than two hours. Impressed with the size and beauty of the fair, they visited exhibits and attended shows all day and into the evening. Ron surveyed the advances in science and medicine. Laura and Sarah headed for the home and food displays. Werner and Dale checked out the latest in farm machinery. Sarah and Eddie admired and petted the animals. Everyone enjoyed a couple rides. One innovation in particular enthralled Eddie—a prototype of a television set.

On the way home he bubbled with excitement. "You wouldn't believe it," he said. "They did a show in one room and we saw it on a screen in a different room. I can't wait until we can have a television set in our home."

"Try to be patient, Honey. It may take a while," Laura cautioned.

When Ron and Tom finished basic training Ron called home. Laura took the call.

"Hi Mom. Guess what, I've got good news."

"Wonderful, Dear. What is it?"

"I applied for training as a medic and I've been approved. This'll help me learn a lot about medical practice."

"I'm happy for you, Honey, but is it dangerous—on the battle front I mean?"

"Not more than other assignments," answered Ron with his fingers crossed.

"Well, I hope not...What about Tom? What'll he be doing?"

"He's been assigned to a mechanical service unit which takes care of big equipment like tanks and trucks."

"I can't help worrying about you boys. I'm sorry I'm such a wimp."

"That's okay Mom. We're doing well. Try not to worry and remember what you always told me, we're in God's hands."

"I'll try, and don't forget how much Dad and I love you. He wants to talk with you now so don't hang up. Goodbye Sweet Potato."

"So long, Mom. I love you."

"I love you very much."

Werner and Ron talked a few minutes covering much the same ground. Then Werner asked, "Do you know where you'll be going?"

"To Europe—probably France. As I mentioned to Mom, I'll be a medic which should give me a lot of valuable experience."

"That's great. We'll be praying for you every day, son."

"Thanks Dad. Give my love to Dale and Sarah and Eddie. I love all you guys."

"We love you too. Bye for now."

Laura and Werner didn't sleep much that night, talking instead about the boys and the war. Trying to reassure Laura Werner said, "Our armed forces have been making steady progress both in Europe and the Pacific. I think the war will be over soon."

Not totally convinced Laura responded, "Let's pray real hard for that."

9. Looking Ahead

The following spring Dale and Eddie replaced Steve in helping their dad seed the oats. They enjoyed their new jobs. Soon Dale would be completing his junior year in high school and Eddie would graduate from the eighth grade. As they drove the tractors they thought of themselves as jockeys riding two powerful horses. On Saturdays they helped all day, but on school days only between four and six in the afternoon. As Dale worked the soil with the disc and harrow, Eddie pulled Werner and the wagon seeder across the field. During such busy times Laura and Sarah did most of the chores. Sweet sixteen and a sophomore, Sarah blossomed into a strong and attractive girl, always eager to be a participant rather than a spectator. Once she even managed to persuade Eddie to let her drive the tractor while *he* helped their mother with the chores.

By this time many farmers had purchased small combines for harvesting oats and consequently the large threshing machines became obsolete. Because Werner no longer needed his team of horses, he donated them to an elderly neighbor farming a small acreage. The neighbor joyfully accepted them.

The Schaub kids were active in high school. All four of of them participated in the music programs; Eddie joined the debate team;

Dale played football. Earlier Ron had played on the basketball team. Eager to earn a little money, Sarah got a part time job as a waitress working on Saturdays. With her pretty blue eyes and blond hair she also fared quite well with tips.

On a cool April day in 1945 the Schaubs and McDonalds received the best news imaginable. Germany had surrendered! In a few weeks both sides would sign a formal peace treaty and before long Ron and Tom would be coming home. Nothing could dampen the joy everyone felt, not even the news received later that Ron had been wounded. As he helped carry a fellow soldier on a stretcher shortly before hostilities ended, a small piece of shrapnel struck his left shoulder. Though not a critical wound, it was serious enough that he received a purple heart. Nevertheless everyone considered the end of the war in Europe a supremely wonderful development.

Hundreds of thousands of troops waited impatiently to board a ship and return home. Tom and Ron didn't get back to the States until early in July. In the meantime life continued routinely on the farm as Dale and Eddie helped Werner with oats combining and cultivating. Then followed a lull in field work. Good timing because the boys arrived home on a four week furlough in mid-July.

What an emotional moment when those two handsome young men in full uniform stepped off the train in Fort Dodge! A number of other servicemen arrived with them. Hugs and kisses rapidly followed as parents, brothers, sisters and friends overflowed with joy. Noticing that Ron's arm was in a sling Laura asked, "How's your shoulder, Sweet Potato?"

"It's okay," he answered. "It's healing well. I'm grateful it didn't hit my right shoulder which would have hindered my right arm in doing medical procedures."

"What will you guys do when your furlough ends?" asked George.

"We're supposed to report to a base in Des Moines," replied Tom. "After that, who knows?"

"Depending on what's going on in the Pacific theater, the Army might ship us over there," added Ron. "Or they might discharge us."

"Well, let's make the most of the time our sons have at home," Werner exclaimed. "I move we have a party!"

"I second the motion," shouted both Betty and Laura in unison.

They invited their friends and neighbors and had a good time eating, drinking, playing horse shoes and just plain visiting. Trying to avoid gory war stories, Tom and Ron described very few of their overseas experiences. During the remainder of their furlough the two soldiers relaxed, visited their friends and helped with farm work when that was needed.

One day Ron and Tom went baling with Dale and Eddie. Norm Johnson had bought a hay and straw baler and needed a crew of four to operate it, one on the tractor and three on the baler. In addition to Steve, Norm frequently hired Dale and Eddie and paid them a penny per bale. That was big money for them, amounting to about four dollars per day. They poked and tied wires and retrieved the bale dividers. It was hot and dusty work with a lot of sweating and itching but the boys felt proud to be considered employees.

Ron wished he could make a few rounds for Eddie and give him a rest, but his left arm was not yet fully functional. Tom said, "Let me do it," and jumped on the machine in Eddie's place. One of the wheels of the baler hit a small hole and it jerked downward, causing Tom to fall forward just as the baler's plunger started descending at high speed. Tom jerked himself back just in the nick of time. The plunger hit the bill of his cap, pushed it down into the hay and flattened it inside a bale. It took place so quickly no one else knew what happened. However Tom was well aware of the close call he experienced and thanked God his head did not suffer the same fate as his cap inside that bale. *"How ironic it would be,"* he thought to himself, *"to come home from the war uninjured and then die in a farm accident while on furlough."* He tried to banish such thoughts from his mind but he did share them with Ron.

When the crew of four plus the two soldiers arrived back at Norm Johnson's place later that day, Norm's wife Claire came running out of the house shouting, "Have you heard the news?"

"No, what news?" they asked.

"A US plane dropped another atomic bomb on a second Japanese city and now Japan is finally willing to surrender. Praise God, the war is over!"

At first the men stood stunned and silent finding the news hard to believe. Finally they began to jump up and down and laugh and hug each other. Tom and Ron shed tears of joy.

People felt frightened when they learned how powerful and destructive the atomic weapons were. Werner expressed the feelings of many when he said, "I hope I'm not here when the next war comes along."

"Isn't it interesting," Ron observed, "that people experienced panic when the war began at Pearl Harbor, and now they're feeling some of the same panic as the war ends at Hiroshima and Nagasaki?"

"That is ironic," Tom concurred.

Events happened faster than anyone expected. The Army discharged Tom and Ron in early September. With help from Army recommendations and the cutting of red tape, they enrolled in the universities they had planned to attend the previous year before the military intervened. In addition they received help with tuition expenses after Congress passed the GI Bill. The two former soldiers were excited that everything fell into place, even though at the last moment.

As planned Ron went to the University of Iowa and majored in pre-medicine and Tom studied mechanical engineering at Iowa State. A year later Dale also enrolled at Iowa State and began a two year program of agricultural studies. He commuted the fifty miles to Ames for his classes which left him free to continue helping his dad on the farm. Although Tom missed Ron, he often saw Dale on the State campus and they became closer friends.

Dale always came home from Ames full of new ideas about the future of farming. Although glad to hear the information Werner sometimes pleaded for a break.

One evening when Dale returned he announced, "Dad, you'd be amazed by what researchers are discovering. One of their visions is to make it unnecessary to spray crops with fertilizers, insecticides and weed killers."

"How could they do that?"

"By putting chemicals directly into the seeds. Of course the seeds would be more expensive, but think how much you would save by not having to spray or cultivate. Also it would be better for the environment."

"Those are exciting ideas," replied Werner, "but I suspect it'll take a while to get them perfected."

"Maybe, maybe not," said Dale.

"Hey, you two!" Laura interrupted. "Is agriculture all you know how to discuss? There are a few more things in life, you know!"

"Sorry Mom, I'll stop." said Dale. "But if you don't mind I'd like to make one suggestion about Grandpa Klaus, okay?"

"Okay."

"I wish he'd hire a commercial company to dig his trenches when he tiles his fields. He's still out there digging them by hand! I know he's strong but he's getting old. I'm afraid he's going to hurt himself seriously one of these days."

"You're right, Dear. Unfortunately he's as stubborn as he is nice. I've talked to him about it many times but I'll try again."

———

That night before they went to sleep Werner and Laura had a long talk about the kids and their future. Laura propped up her pillow and leaned back. "You know, Honey," she said, "I'm glad Dale likes his college classes so much. It seems to make him feel more involved in everything."

"That's true," said Werner. "What makes me happy is that he seems committed to farming."

"I hope that means he'll work with you until you retire. Then he could take over the farm himself."

"That would be great. I'd never want to sell this place."

"Especially after all we went through to get it," mused Laura.

"That's right. But you know what? I'm happy for Ron too. Since he was a little kid he wanted to be a doctor like my father. Now it seems his dream may come true."

"What a gift that is. He's intelligent and he cares about people. I'm sure he'll be an excellent physician...This may surprise you. Sarah said she'd like to become a nurse."

"I am surprised!" replied Werner. "She once told me she wanted to marry a farmer."

"Well, she's only seventeen and not sure about anything yet. The last time she and I talked she said she'd like to be a farmer's wife during the week and a nurse on weekends. You know Sarah, she always goes for broke."

"But she usually gets what she wants...Since you surprised me about Sarah, let's see if I can surprise you about Eddie. Recently he expressed to me some interest in the ministry."

"Sorry to disappoint you but yes, he mentioned that to me too. Isn't he quite young to make such a serious decision?"

"Well he *is* fifteen," said Werner. "He told me he'd like to do what his Grandpa Schaub's brother Harry is doing in Nebraska, and Uncle Harry's been a pastor for more than thirty five years."

"He must definitely have some interest," replied Laura. "If it continues maybe we should talk with Pastor Larson and seek his advice."

"Sounds right. I'm glad we had this talk tonight, Sweetheart. It's always nice to learn a few things you didn't know about your own kids!"

Werner leaned over and gave Laura a little kiss. "Now I want to change the subject and ask a question. I'd like to drive to Sioux City and see my parents this weekend. Would you and Sarah and Eddie be interested in going along?"

"It's been quite a while since we visited them. Is that why you want to go?"

"That's one reason, but I also want to pay back the loan my dad gave us for a down payment on the farm."

"It's been over a decade since he made that loan. Do you think he still expects to be repaid?"

"Maybe not, but God has been good to us in recent years and I'd like to pay Dad back."

"So we can afford to do it, right?"

"Yes, I believe we can. During the war years the weather, the crops, and especially the prices have been excellent. We've paid off a lot of our debts in full and now we have only the farm mortgage payment to make each month. We can handle that without a problem. Do you realize how happy I am to be able to say that?"

"I sure do, Honey. I'll be happy to go with you to see your parents, and I'm sure Sarah and Eddie will be glad to go too. It'll be fun for all of us. I'll bet your dad has more than enough time for a visit now that he's retired from his practice at the hospital."

"You're absolutely right. Now let me confess to you one of my less noble motives for the trip to Sioux City. I can't wait to see the look of shock and surprise on my dad's face when I hand him that check!"

"Werner Schaub, you're a devil! But then I must confess, I can't wait to see his face either!"

Epilog

"Ladies and gentlemen, please buckle your seat belts. We'll be landing shortly in Fort Dodge, Iowa," announced the flight attendant. Asleep in his seat, Dr. Ron Schaub did not stir. Tapping him lightly on the shoulder the attendant said, "Wake up, Sir, we're preparing to land."

Ron responded slowly. Gradually he became aware that he had been dreaming while in a deep sleep. It surprised him when he realized he had relived much of his childhood during his dream. *"How was it possible,"* he mused, *"that he could experience so clearly in his sleep many things that happened in the 1930's and 40's, and here it was 1990 again!"*

When he got off the plane Dale was there to greet him. A happy reunion followed, celebrated with a bear hug. "How's my favorite agriculturalist?" asked Ron with a smile.

"Just fine, Doctor, and how are your patients?" Both laughed and headed for Dale's car.

Though it had been only two years since they had seen one another, each thought the other had changed somewhat in appearance. Over six feet tall, Dale still sported dark blond hair and side burns. Ron seemed a little older and more gray but distinguished looking.

"I'm glad you came back for a visit even though you weren't able to bring Susan this time," said Dale. "Mom and Dad are so eager to see you."

"I can imagine...I want to tell you how grateful I am that you helped them enter an assisted living facility. Many older people aren't able to get into a place like that or don't have enough money, and frequently they end up lonely and ill both physically and mentally."

Because Laura and Werner lived in a small two room apartment in the facility, the family waited in a large lounge. When Dale and Ron arrived pandemonium broke out with shrieks, laughter, hugs and kisses. Most of the Schaub clan had come including Sarah's and Dale's spouses and children and grandchildren. The entire group enjoyed a wonderful if boisterous visit.

"It's so wonderful to see you," said Laura, squeezing Ron's hand. "Are Susan and the girls okay?"

"They're fine. The girls are busy with their families and Susan is attending a work conference in Columbus, Ohio. They said I should be sure to give you their love."

After things settled down Werner and Laura, who were now in their mid-eighties, announced that they would like to share something. Werner began by saying, "Since most of our family is together today, Mother and I want to tell all of you that we're very proud of you. Not only have you been great "kids" but you've made your lives count in the world: Ron with his medical practice; Dale as my farming partner; and Sarah as the best nurse in Webster County."

"Don't forget Eddie," continued Laura. "It's hard to believe that he's been a pastor for thirty four years, first in Nebraska and now in Ohio. I'm glad he and his family are now in Columbus, not too far from Ron."

"That's right," said Ron. "His family and mine manage to get together occasionally. Cleveland and Columbus aren't far apart.

"One more thing," said Werner. "Without getting too emotional, Mother and I want to tell each and every one of you that we love you with all our heart, and we hope you'll visit us whenever it's convenient for you."

It was a moving moment when Werner, who had always had difficulty telling his children that he loved them, finally did so with powerful sincerity and emotion.

The next few days Ron visited at the homes of Sarah and Dale, got reacquainted with his nephews and nieces and their kids, and caught up with what was going on in their lives. At night he slept at Dale's remodeled home, the same house in which he grew up fifty years earlier.

Each evening he made a trip back to town for a special visit with his parents alone. Although they seemed happy in their apartment, they indicated they missed the roominess of the old farmhouse and also having loved ones around them. Laura said, "Lots of nice people live here but I'm still lonely sometimes." Her words made Ron feel sad. But on the other hand it was clear his parents believed they were lucky to be there and appreciated the good care they were receiving. That helped Ron feel a little better.

He saved one day to reconnect with his friend Tom who still lived and worked in Ames. They were excited to see each other and spent several hours walking around the university campus, visiting and reminiscing.

After a brief but thoroughly enjoyable stay, Ron packed his bag and prepared to return home. Once again Dale provided transportation. As they drove to the airport Ron said, "Fort Dodge surely has changed over the past fifty years. Main Street seems more quiet and lonely, nothing like the bustling strip we used to cruise on Saturday nights when we were kids, remember?"

"I sure do. One factor is that a few shopping malls have sprung up on the east edge of town and a number of the stores have moved out there from Main Street. It's true, the character of the city has changed."

"Most cities are experiencing the same thing, I suppose," Ron stated. "In one way it may be good—all in the name of progress as they say. But it also makes me sad. Some valuable things get lost in the process."

"Do you recall that old shop where we used to get milk shakes?" asked Dale. "Well, that's gone for sure."

"And forever," added Ron.

When the brothers separated at the airport they gave each other one more bear hug and said goodbye. "Come soon and visit us in Cleveland, " said Ron as he walked toward the small plane warming up its engines. As the plane lifted into the air Ron looked forward to seeing Susan and his daughters again. Even getting back to work in his medical practice seemed appealing at that moment.

Ron glanced out the window and looked down. There once again he saw the same beautiful view he had seen on his way *toward* Fort Dodge several days earlier—thousands of green rows of corn and soy beans racing across the fields below. And once again he remembered the wonderful times he and his family enjoyed long ago between those rows.

Smiling and closing his eyes, Ron said softly to himself, *"Maybe if I fall asleep I'll have another beautiful dream..."*

19386744R00068

Made in the USA
Lexington, KY
16 December 2012